Grammar Workbook

Tip Top Education

An Intro to Advanced Grammar

- Sentences
- Parts of Speech
- Phrases and Clauses
- Verbals
- Verb Tenses
- Problem Verbs
- Punctuation
- Sentence Writing
- And More...
- Answer Key Included

INTRODUCTION

The text *Grammar Workbook* is a grammar text for students that are ready for an introduction to the study of advanced grammar. The lessons are well explained and easy to understand. This workbook will provide students with a solid foundation in basic grammatical topics. Because the text introduces the basics of phrases, clauses, gerunds, participles, and other advanced topics, this text can also be used by older students to review these areas.

This workbook covers sentences, the eight parts of speech, clauses and phrases, the five sentence patterns, and the basics of punctuation.

Initially students learn about sentences, giving them a framework within which to study grammar. They study subjects and predicates, the four types of sentences, independent and dependent clauses, and compound and complex sentences. Occasionally, in the sentence writing sections, students are asked to compose sentences that imitate model sentences given.

In addition to covering the fundamentals of the eight parts of speech, students learn about possessive nouns, appositives, the principal parts of verbs, verb forms, and the difference between prepositions and adverbs.

After covering the parts of speech, students study the five basic sentence patterns. By doing so, they review the parts of speech and learn how words function in a sentence, creating the different patterns. Students learn that the specific kinds of subjects, verbs, extra nouns, pronouns, or adjectives determine the pattern of the sentence.

After obtaining a better understanding of words, phrases, clauses, and sentence patterns, students review the basics of punctuation.

The topics in this text, *Grammar Workbook*, are organized to build upon one another while simultaneously reviewing basic concepts. At the beginning of each lesson, students are given explanatory information that is simplified yet more thorough than most modern texts.

To create this grammar workbook, our team of writers has reviewed several older public domain textbooks and used these more advanced books as the model for the text, *Grammar Workbook*. The end result is a challenging, yet easy to understand, modern text that prepares students for advanced grammar.

ISBN-13: 978-1517414610

CONTENTS

SENTENCES

A sentence is a group of words that **expresses a complete thought**. When words are joined together, they must tell something about a person or thing and express a complete thought to form a **sentence**.

- A sentence **begins with a capital letter**.
- A sentence **ends with a punctuation mark**.

The rain fell fast**.**

A sentence consists of two parts. Whom or what the sentence tells about is called **the subject**, and what it tells about the subject is called **the predicate.** A complete sentence has both a **subject** and a **predicate**.

- To find the **subject**, ask yourself: Whom or what does the sentence tell about?
- To find the **predicate**, ask yourself: What does the sentence tell about the subject?

Columbus sailed across the ocean.

Whom or what is the sentence about?	Columbus	subject
What does it tell about the subject?	sailed across the ocean	predicate

Mary went to the store.

Who or what went to the store?	Mary	subject
What does the sentence tell about Mary?	went to the store	predicate

EXERCISE 1: Underline the groups of words that are complete sentences.

1. President George Washington lived at Mt. Vernon.
2. The tops of distant mountains.
3. The daisy is yellow.
4. Down the long, narrow street.
5. Rosebushes heavy with blossoms.
6. The mist rose from the meadows.
7. To hit the nail on the head.
8. Modern ships cross the Atlantic in five days.
9. My favorite novel.
10. *To Kill a Mockingbird* is my favorite novel.

EXERCISE 2: Complete the following sentences by adding a subject to each of the predicates.

1. ______________________ is a large city.
2. ______________________ is the President of the United States.
3. ______________________ discovered America.
4. ______________________ is sailing into the harbor.

EXERCISE 3: Complete the following sentences by adding a predicate to each of the subjects.

1. The Mississippi River ____________________________________.
2. Maple sugar ____.
3. The state of Texas ______________________________________.
4. An island ____.
5. A river ____.
6. The Rocky Mountains ____________________________________.

EXERCISE 4: Draw a vertical line between the subject and the predicate of the following sentences. On the lines provided, compose sentences of your own that imitate the model sentences.

Ex.: The house of the merchant **|** was built of brick.
The home of the architect was constructed of cardboard.

1. Evangeline cried.

____

____

2. Vast meadows stretched over the horizon.

____

____

3. The chimney filled with smoke.

____

____

4. The young woman walked proudly through the village.

____

____

SIMPLE SUBJECT AND SIMPLE PREDICATE

The **subject** of a sentence tells us whom or what the sentence is about. The **predicate** of a sentence tells us what the subject does.

A sentence that consists of one subject and one predicate is a **simple sentence**. It may, however, have adjectives, adverbs, articles, prepositions, and other words in it to make it more informative. Often one word in the subject of the sentence makes up the **simple subject**, and one or two words in the predicate make up the **simple predicate**. To find which noun is the simple subject of the sentence and which verb is the simple predicate of the sentence, remove the modifiers, including adjectives, adverbs, and prepositional phrases.

A rolling stone gathers no moss.

What gathers no moss?	stone
What is the sentence telling us the stone does?	gathers

The north wind sings a doleful song.

What sings a doleful song?	wind
What is the sentence telling us the wind does?	sings

EXERCISE 5: Find the simple subject and simple predicate (verb) of each sentence. Underline the simple subject once and the simple predicate (verb) twice.

1. The little boy rode his scooter around the block.
2. Aunt Susie bakes the best cakes.
3. Several children from the neighborhood were playing near the fountain.
4. Many different kinds of monkeys live at the zoo.
5. Video games can shorten your attention span.

EXERCISE 6: Draw a vertical line between the subject and the predicate of the following sentences.

1. The beautiful princess | quickly climbed over the hill.
2. The astronaut donned his spacesuit.
3. The children slept quietly while the parents drove through the night.
4. The dog jumped into the river to save his master.
5. My grandparents successfully completed a twenty-six mile marathon last month.

ORDER OF SUBJECT AND PREDICATE

Notice the position of the **subject** in each of these sentences:

1. **Father flew to Chicago.**
2. **Down went the flag.**
3. **During the storm, they sang.**

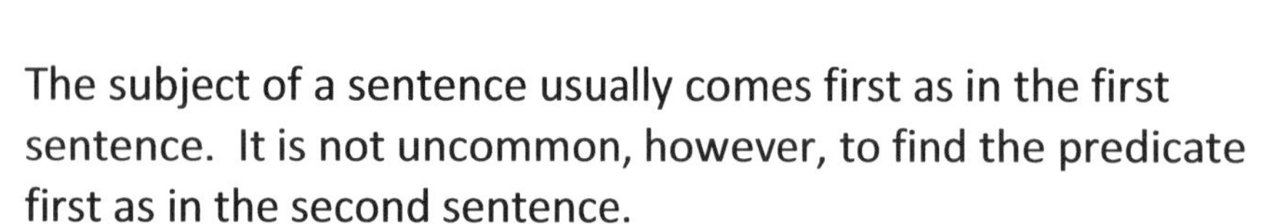

The subject of a sentence usually comes first as in the first sentence. It is not uncommon, however, to find the predicate first as in the second sentence.

When the entire subject comes first, the sentence is arranged in the **natural order**. Any other arrangement is called the **inverted order**.

EXERCISE 7: Rearrange each of the following sentences so that the whole subject comes first.

1. Over the hill the farm boy goes.

____

____

2. Up the chimney roared the fire.

____

____

3. Above their heads towered a lofty mountain.

____

____

4. Down came the soft and silent snow.

____

____

5. A rare old plant is the ivy green.

____

____

TYPES OF SENTENCES

If we examine the sentences below, we find that the first makes a **statement**, the second asks a **question**, the third expresses a **command**, and the fourth implies **strong feeling**.

1. **Neil Armstrong was a great explorer.**
2. **Have you finished your lesson?**
3. **Stay off the grass.**
4. **That stung!**

These four types of sentences are declarative, interrogative, imperative, and exclamatory.

Declarative Sentences make statements.

The sun rises in the east.

Interrogative Sentences ask a question.

What are you doing?

Imperative Sentences express commands.

Don't give up the ship. Help me!

Exclamatory Sentences express strong feelings.

The baby is so beautiful!

EXERCISE 8: On the lines below, write the sentence type; notice how each sentence is punctuated. Beneath each sentence, compose a sentence of your own that imitates the model sentence.

Declarative Interrogative Imperative Exclamatory

1. Neil Armstrong was the first person to walk on the moon. ____________________

____

____

2. What a great time we had last night! ______________________________

____

____

3. What causes the change of seasons? ____________________

____

____

4. Write your lesson on ruled paper. ____________________

____

____

5. I cut my finger! ____________________

____

____

6. O wind, that sings so loud a song! ____________________

____

____

7. The dogs are barking again. ____________________

____

____

8. Who has seen the wind? ____________________

____

____

9. Dare to do right! Dare to be true! ____________________

____

____

10. You have a work that no other can do. ____________________

____

____

DECLARATIVE AND INTERROGATIVE SENTENCES

What kind of sentence is each of the following—**declarative** or **interrogative**?

1. James is singing.
2. Is James singing?
3. Where were you?
4. James has arrived.
5. Has James arrived?
6. Do you hear?

The main differences between declarative and interrogative sentences are:

- Thought: Declarative sentences tell. Interrogative sentences ask.
- Form: Declarative sentences end with periods, and the subject usually comes first. Interrogative sentences end with question marks, and either the whole predicate or a part of the predicate usually comes first.

EXERCISE 9: Change each of the following sentences. Change the declarative sentences to interrogative sentences. Change the interrogative sentences to declarative sentences. Add or remove language as necessary to make the sentence grammatically correct.

Ex.: Arbor Day originated in Nebraska.
Did Arbor Day originate in Nebraska?

1. De Soto discovered the Mississippi River.

____

____

2. The first school in Chicago was opened in 1816.

____

____

3. Patrick Henry was an eloquent speaker.

____

____

4. Is New Orleans sometimes called the Crescent City?

____

____

IMPERATIVE SENTENCES

When a teacher tells students to, "Open your textbooks," he commands them to do something. The predicate is *open your textbooks*. The subject is the understood *you*.

Open your textbooks.
Do not quit.
Honor your parents.
You read next.

Imperative sentences and declarative sentences differ in the following ways:

- **In thought**

Imperative sentences do not give information but express a command.

- **In form**

The subject is *you*, and since the sentence makes sense without it, the *you* is often omitted.

EXERCISE 10: Rewrite the sentences below. Add the understood you in parenthesis. Draw a vertical line between the subject and predicate of each sentence. Circle the simple predicate.

Return at five o'clock.
Ex.: (You) **|** return at five o'clock.

1. Aim at perfection in everything.

____

2. Do not look a gift horse in the mouth.

____

3. Don't give up the ship.

____

4. Now, tell me all about the performance.

____

5. Overcome evil with good.

____

EXCLAMATORY SENTENCES

Examine the following sentences:

1. How awesome your new car is!
2. What a terrible fire this is!

These sentences are not statements, questions, or commands. They are purely **exclamatory.** Such sentences are usually introduced by how or what, and the subject and predicate often have the inverted order.

The above sentences are exclamatory in **form** as well as in **sense**. There are other sentences that are exclamatory in sense but not in form.

Most sentences may be made exclamatory if uttered with sufficient feeling.

1. We are lost!
2. What do you mean!
3. Stop that thief!
4. How strong Harry looks!

As far as **form** is concerned, sentence 1 is declarative, 2 is interrogative, and 3 is imperative, yet each is considered exclamatory in **sense**, as is shown by the punctuation.

EXERCISE 11: Classify the following sentences. Write the type of each sentence on the line provided.

Declarative   Interrogative   Imperative   Exclamatory

1. How small these apples are! ________________________

2. I can't believe it! ________________________

3. Insects visit flowers in search of honey.

____

4. Oases furnish resting places for travelers.

____

5. It was a cold, wet, rainy day. ________________________

6. Close the blinds, please. ________________________

7. Have you finished your geography homework?

____

- **SENTENCE WRITING PRACTICE 1:** Compose two of each type of sentence—declarative, interrogative, imperative, and exclamatory.

Declarative Sentences make statements. The sun rises in the east.
Interrogative Sentences ask a question. What are you doing?
Imperative Sentences express commands. Don't give up the ship. Help me!
Exclamatory Sentences express strong feelings. The baby is so beautiful!

1. ______________________________

____

____

2. ______________________________

____

____

3. ______________________________

____

____

4. ______________________________

____

____

5. ______________________________

____

____

6. ______________________________

____

____

7. ______________________________

____

____

8. ______________________________

____

____

INDEPENDENT CLAUSES

A **clause** is a group of words that contains a subject and a verb. Clauses can be independent or dependent. Independent clauses can stand alone. A simple sentence is also called an **independent clause** because it can stand alone. A **dependent clause** cannot stand alone.

An independent clause can, however, have **compound parts**. It can have more than one subject, predicate, adjective, or phrase. In a compound subject, predicate, adjective, or phrase, the two parts are usually joined with **and,** but can also be joined with **or** or sometimes **but.**

The **parents** and their **children** | *are* eating ice cream. 2 subjects + 1 predicate
(When compound subjects are joined by *and*, the verb is typically plural.)

The youngest daughter | **went** to sleep and **had** a dream. 1 subject + 2 predicates

When you have several simple sentences with the same subject, you can join them together to make your writing less repetitive.

The family went shopping.
The family ate ice cream.
The family watched a movie.

The family | went shopping, ate ice cream, and watched a movie.
(A simple sentence with a compound predicate.)

The compound verbs in the predicate share one subject—*family*.

When you have several simple sentences with the same predicate, you can join them together as well.

Bobby went to school.
Karen went to school.
Hunter went to school.

Bobby, Karen, and Hunter | went to school.
(A simple sentence with a compound subject.)

The compound subjects share one verb in the predicate—*went*.

EXERCISE 12: Place a vertical line (|) between the complete subject and the complete predicate of each of the following sentences. On the line beneath each sentence, write compound subject or compound predicate.

1. England and Wales have extensive copper mines.

____

2. Susie ate ice cream and enjoyed the summer night.

____

3. A fifteen-piece band played and marched in the parade.

____

4. No tree or shrub grew upon the surface of the island.

____

5. More than four hundred people gathered and piled into the auditorium.

____

EXERCISE 13: By using compound elements, condense each of the following groups of sentences into one sentence.

1. We went over the bridge. We went down the lane. We went through the meadow.

____

____

2. The boys enjoyed the camping trip. The girls enjoyed the camping trip. The parents enjoyed the camping trip.

____

____

3. The day was blustery. The day was cold. The day was generally disagreeable.

____

____

4. The people shouted. The people waved their arms. The people tried to express their joy.

____

____

COMPOUND SENTENCES

A sentence may consist of two or more independent clauses. Sentences that contain two or more independent clauses are called **compound sentences**.

Compound sentences can be combined in three ways:

, coordinating conjunction
Congress | passed the bill**, and** the President | signed it.

; conjunctive adverb,
Brag | is a good dog**; however,** Holdfast | is better.

;
An hour | passed**;** the teacher | awoke.

Coordinating Conjunctions	Conjunctive Adverbs
for, and, nor, but, or, yet, so	consequently, therefore, however, nevertheless, thus, hence, henceforth

EXERCISE 14: For each sentence, underline the independent clauses. Circle either the punctuation or the punctuation and conjunction joining the two clauses.

1. The night is dark, and I am far from home.
2. The shallows murmur, but the deeps are dumb.
3. The piper advanced; the children followed.
4. Hunger is the best sauce, and fatigue is the best pillow.
5. The students studied their lessons; therefore, they were ready for the quiz.

➢ **SENTENCE WRITING PRACTICE 2:** On the lines below and on the following page, write three simple sentences. Follow the directions given.

1. Compose a simple sentence with a simple subject and a simple predicate.

____

____

2. Compose a simple sentence with a compound subject and a simple predicate.

3. Compose a simple sentence with a simple subject and a compound predicate.

➢ **SENTENCE WRITING PRACTICE 3:** On the lines provided, compose sentences of your own that imitate the model sentences below.

1. He feared trouble, and trouble came.

   Ex: She desired solitude, but solitude vanished. (Create your own.)

2. The shallow waters murmur, but the deep oceans are silent.

3. The piper advanced; the children followed.

4. Hunger is the best sauce, and fatigue is the best pillow.

COMPLEX SENTENCES

Sentences that contain an independent clause and one or more dependent (subordinate) clauses are called **complex sentences**.

Examine the following sentence:
Lock the stable before the horse is stolen.

The above sentence consists of two clauses:

(1) Lock the stable
(2) before the horse is stolen.

The first clause expresses the main thought of the sentence; it is complete by itself. This clause is called an **independent clause.**

The second clause does not express an independent thought but only tells when the stable should be locked. The second clause modifies the verb *lock* like an adverb. It is a **subordinate** or **dependent clause**.

Independent Clause:

- Expresses a complete thought. Ex. ***I will come*** when you send for me.

Subordinate or Dependent Clause

- Is used like a noun, an adjective, or an adverb.
- Cannot stand alone. Ex. I will come ***when you send for me.***
- Begins with a subordinating conjunction. Ex. I will come ***when*** you send for me.

Subordinate Conjunctions

after	once	until
although	provided that	when
as	rather than	whenever
because	since	where
before	so that	whereas
even if	than	wherever
even though	that	whether
if	though	while
in order that	unless	why

Note: When the dependent clause begins a sentence, a comma is required between the two clauses. If the dependent clause is at the end, there is no comma.

We find the most weeds where the soil is richest.
Where the soil is richest, we find the most weeds.

EXERCISE 15: Tell whether each sentence is simple or complex.

1. He smiled when he saw me. ____________________
2. A fair face may hide a foul heart. ____________________
3. Hold the horse until I return. ____________________
4. Drowning men catch at straws. ____________________
5. The longest way around is the shortest way home. ____________________
6. He is a fine man although he is sad. ____________________
7. Inventors make many efforts before they succeed. ____________________
8. Unless you put on your coat, you will freeze. ____________________
9. While you were away, three marketers called. ____________________
10. The students failed because they did not study. ____________________

EXERCISE 16: Circle the independent clause in each sentence. Underline the dependent clause. Look for the subordinating conjunctions to help you locate the dependent clauses.

1. She has lived there since she was born.

2. As the line tightened, the trout leaped out of the water.

3. As he approached the stream, his heart began to thump.

4. She pushed up her sleeves as though she were going to fight for the champion's belt.

5. The swift phantom of the desert was gone before we could get our heads out of the window.

6. The goods that were not sold were packed away.

7. After I had eaten my dinner, I went out for a walk.

COMMON AND PROPER NOUNS

A **noun** is a word that names a person, place, thing, or idea.

Person	Place	Thing	Idea
parent police officer clown	beach school zoo	telephone banana remote control	happiness love future

The word **noun** means name. Nouns include:

- All objects that we can observe with our senses—see, hear, taste, touch, or smell.
- All objects that we can think about.

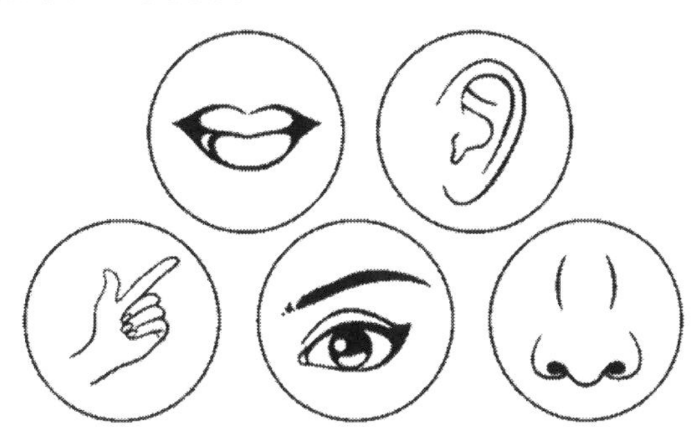

Rules:

1. A **proper noun** is the name of a particular person, place, thing, or idea:
   George, Chicago, April, Catholicism
2. Begin every proper noun with a capital letter. Note that all words that make up the proper noun are capitalized, e.g. **George Brown**, **New York**, or **Chicago Tribune**.
3. A **common noun** is the name of any one of a class of persons, places, things, or ideas:
   boy, city, month, religion

EXERCISE 17: IDENTIFYING NOUNS: Circle the nouns in the sentences below. On the line, write see, hear, taste, touch, smell, or think. (Complete on the following page.)

1. The house is beautiful. ______________________

2. The sound of the music was terrible. ______________________

____

3. A gentle breeze was blowing. ______________________

4. The fragrance of these flowers is delightful. ______________________

5. The strength of the gorilla is very great. ______________________

6. The air resounded with the songs of the birds. ______________________

7. The clatter of the cars annoyed him. ______________________

8. The sleigh bells were ringing. ______________________

9. John, my brother, can learn his lessons in an hour. ______________________

10. Good health is better than wealth. ______________________

EXERCISE 18: COMMON NOUNS: Write a common noun that corresponds to each.

Ex.	Cuba	island
1.	Rockies	________
2.	Alabama	________
3.	November	________
4.	Baltimore	________
5.	Thursday	________

PROPER NOUNS: Write a proper noun for each noun.

Ex.	general	Robert E. Lee
1.	street	________
2.	peninsula	________
3.	book	________
4.	gulf	________
5.	mountain	________

PLURAL NOUNS

To show that there is more than one noun, we often add the letter *-s* to the end of a noun to make it a plural noun; however, some words require special changes be made to the root word before we can add an *-s*.

NOUNS THAT END IN A CONSONANT + *Y* The *y* is changed to *i*, and *-es* is added.

New York is a large city. **New York and Chicago are large cities.**

The singular noun *city* ends in the letter *y* preceded by the consonant *t.* In the plural noun *cities*, *y* has been changed to *i*, and *-es* has been added. Note that this rule only applies when the *y* at the end of the word is directly preceded by a consonant. When the *y* at the end of the word is preceded by a vowel, there is no change when pluralizing the noun.

SINGULAR	PLURAL	SINGULAR	PLURAL
baby	babies	lady	ladies
kitty	kitties	army	armies
daisy	daisies	lily	lilies

NOUNS THAT END IN *O* Adding *-es* to the single form of the noun.

Leonidas was a hero. **His Spartans were heroes.**

The singular noun *hero* ends in *o* and is preceded by a consonant. Such nouns usually form the plural by adding *-es* to the singular form (but not always!).

SINGULAR	PLURAL	SINGULAR	PLURAL
echo	echoes	tomato	tomatoes
potato	potatoes	volcano	volcanoes
piano	pianos	garbanzo	garbanzos

NOUNS THAT END IN *SS, SH, CH, X or Z* Adding *-es* to the singular form.

Put the brush on the table. **My brushes are dirty.**

The singular noun *brush* ends in *h* and is preceded by a consonant. Such nouns usually form the plural by adding *-es* to the singular form.

SINGULAR	PLURAL	SINGULAR	PLURAL
fuss	fusses	loss	losses
bush	bushes	radish	radishes
church	churches	watch	watches
box	boxes	hex	hexes
buzz	buzzes	spritz	spritzes

- **SENTENCE WRITING PRACTICE 4:** Writing sentences with plural nouns. If necessary, use the tables on the previous page to help you.

Write two sentences, each using the plural form of a noun that ends in *y.*

1. ____

____

2. ____

____

Write two sentences, each using the plural form of a noun that ends in *o*.

1. ____

____

2. ____

____

Write two sentences, each using the plural form of a noun that ends in *h*.

1. ____

____

2. ____

____

NOUNS THAT CHANGE *F* TO *V* — Change the f to v, add -es

The leaf was yellow. **The leaves were yellow.**

In special cases involving a singular noun ending in *f* or *fe*, the *f* or *fe* is changed to a *v*, and *–es* is added. (Note: The plural of *chief* is *chiefs*.)

SINGULAR	PLURAL	SINGULAR	PLURAL	SINGULAR	PLURAL
knife	knives	half	halves	self	selves
life	lives	calf	calves	shelf	shelves
wife	wives	wolf	wolves	loaf	loaves

NOUNS THAT DO NOT ADD *–S* — Nouns that don't follow the rules

Twelve inches make one foot. Three feet make one yard.

Some nouns are irregular and do not follow the standard rules of pluralization. Which noun is used in the singular form in the first sentence and in the plural form in the second? (*foot*)

SINGULAR	PLURAL	SINGULAR	PLURAL	SINGULAR	PLURAL
man	men	foot	feet	goose	geese
woman	women	child	children	ox	oxen
mouse	mice	tooth	teeth	person	people

NOUNS THAT DO NOT CHANGE FORM — Nouns that stay the same

There was one sheep in the pen. The farmer had ten sheep.

A few nouns have the same form for the singular and the plural such as one deer or four deer.

Note: Letters, figures, and signs are made plural by sometimes adding an*–s*. If the letter is lowercase or if there is possible confusion, use an apostrophe.

Dot your i'*s* and cross your t'*s*.
Dot your I's and cross your Ts.
The 1990s flew by.

- **SENTENCE WRITING PRACTICE 5:** Writing sentences with plural nouns.

Write two sentences, each using the plural form of a noun that ends in *f* or *fe*.

1. ____

____

2. ____

____

Write two sentences, each using the plural form of a noun that does not add *s*.

1. ____

____

2. ____

____

Write two sentences, one using the singular form of a noun that does not change form, and the other using the plural form of the same noun.

1. ____

____

2. ____

____

EXERCISE 19: Write the plural form of the following singular nouns.

SINGULAR	PLURAL	SINGULAR	PLURAL
1. church	__________	6. leaf	__________
2. tooth	__________	7. city	__________
3. story	__________	8. army	__________
4. piano	__________	9. monkey	__________
5. voice	__________	10. thief	__________

ABSTRACT AND CONCRETE NOUNS

Words such as *goodness, honesty, strength,* or *activity* are ideas or qualities that cannot be seen, heard, smelled, tasted, or touched. As a general rule, names of things that cannot be perceived by the senses are **abstract nouns**; names of things that can be perceived by the senses are **concrete nouns**.

Most abstract nouns are derived from other words:

- From adjectives
  royal ***royalty***
- From nouns
  boy ***boyhood***
- From verbs
  attract ***attraction***

EXERCISE 20: In the following sentences, underline the abstract nouns.

1. The whiteness of this paper is remarkable.
2. Washington's goodness was known by all.
3. Wisdom should always be pursued.
4. Pride goeth before destruction.
5. Beauty is its own reason for existence.
6. Education is the act of gaining knowledge.
7. Always speak the truth in love.
8. We should always practice moderation and relaxation.

EXERCISE 21: For each noun below, write *A* if the noun is abstract and *C* if the noun is concrete.

________	weariness	________	resistance
________	growth	________	sidewalk
________	child	________	carpet
________	childhood	________	boy
________	sickness	________	truth
________	television	________	telephone
________	anger	________	bacteria

COLLECTIVE NOUNS

Certain nouns name groups (collections) of persons, animals, places, or things--*audience, herd, United States*. These nouns are called **collective nouns**.

Collective nouns may be singular or plural. If the collective noun is referring to a group acting together as one, the collective noun is singular. If the collective noun is referring to the individuals in a group, who are acting independently of one another, the collective noun is plural.

My entire *family* is coming for Christmas. *Family* is one group doing the same thing.
My *family* are coming one at a time. *Family* is individuals doing different things.

EXERCISE 22: In the following sentences choose the correct form of the verb.

1. A herd of horses (was, were) seen on the desert.
2. The committee (is, are) meeting today.
3. The audience (was, were) very responsive to the performance.
4. Our football team (is, are) practicing hard to win.
5. The flock of geese (was, were) flying northward.
6. The orchestra (is, are) tuning their instruments.
7. A class of worried students (was, were) comparing notes before the test.

➢ **SENTENCE WRITING PRACTICE 6:** On the lines below (and on the following page), compose sentences using the collective nouns given. Create your sentences so that the nouns act as one group doing the same activity.

1. team

____

____

____

____

2. set

3. family

- **SENTENCE WRITING PRACTICE 7:** On the lines provided, compose sentences using the same collective nouns as in the previous exercise. This time create your sentences so that the collective nouns refer to the individuals in a group who are acting independently of one another.

1. team

2. set

3. family

POSSESSIVE NOUNS

Singular Possessive Nouns **This is the girl's book.**

The girl's book means the book is owned by one girl. An apostrophe and *s* **('s)** are added to the singular noun *girl* to show **ownership** or **possession**.

Plural Possessive Nouns **These are the girls' books.**

The *girls' books* means the books are owned by the girls. An **apostrophe** (') alone is added to the plural noun *girls* to show **possession.** *Girls* is a plural noun that ends in *s,* and the apostrophe follows the pluralizing s at the end of the word.

EXERCISE 23: Study the following groups of words. On the line, write whether the possessive noun is singular or plural.

1. The chef's knives ______________________
2. The horses' tails ______________________
3. The cat's tongue ______________________
4. The ladies' purses ______________________
5. The baby's bib ______________________

Other Plural Possessive Nouns **Bring me the children's books.**

The children's books means the books are owned by the children. Notice that *children* is a plural noun that does not end in *s.* An **apostrophe** and **s** are added to the plural noun children to show **possession**.

EXERCISE 24: Study the following groups of words. On the line, write whether the possessive noun is singular or plural.

1. The child's toy ______________________
2. The men's tickets ______________________
3. The sheep's fleeces ______________________
4. The woman's hat ______________________
5. The fireman's pay ______________________

APPOSITIVES

An **appositive** is a noun, noun phrase, or noun clause that renames or explains some noun or pronoun that is near it.

John Jones, the grocer, has failed.
John Jones has failed.

In the first sentence above, the noun *grocer* is added to the subject to explain which John Jones is being discussed. The noun *grocer* is an appositive.

- If the main sentence makes sense without the appositive, use commas.

The first president of the United States was popular.	Clear
The first president of the United States, George Washington, was popular.	Commas

- If the main sentence needs the appositive, do not add commas.

The popular teacher is retiring this year.	Unclear
The popular teacher Mrs. Smith is retiring this year.	No commas

- An appositive may be a clause.

Mr. Smith is also retiring.	Clear
Mr. Smith, the man who teaches math, is also retiring.	Commas

EXERCISE 25: The sentences below contain appositives. Underline the appositives, and add commas if needed.

1. One boy Charles White was absent.

2. We went fishing yesterday Frank and I.

3. Elias Howe the inventor of the sewing machine was once a poor man.

4. The children were found in a wretched house a mere shed near the river.

5. The girl who sang the national anthem is named Rebecca.

6. This is Mrs. Morgan a member of the school committee.

7. My friend George is coming for a visit this weekend.

➢ **SENTENCE WRITING PRACTICE 8:** For each word or phrase given, compose a sentence with an appositive.

1. lawyer

Mr. Whitcom, the lawyer, is out of town.

2. Mrs. Smith

3. first American president

4. Sojourner Truth

5. my sister

6. Washington D. C.

VERBS

A **verb** is a word that shows action or links a subject to its predicate.

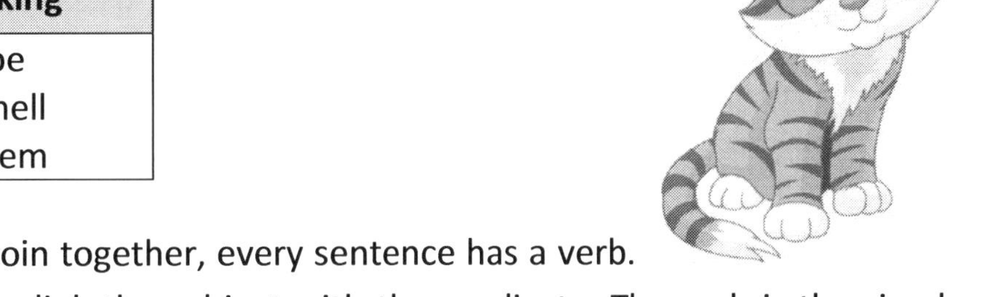

Action	Linking
dance	be
sob	smell
think	seem

No matter how many words we join together, every sentence has a verb.
Verbs tell us about the subject or link the subject with the predicate. The verb is the simple predicate of a sentence.

Cats *see* in the dark.
The withered leaves *fall*.
Toads *have* bright eyes.
The sailor *climbs* the mast.

Most verbs show action: He **mowed** the lawn.
A few show being or state: Lions **are** in Africa.
Some verbs link two words together: He **grew** tall. He **is** tall.

- Action verbs:

  include such words as:

jump	**dash**	**explode**
have	**skip**	**throw**
say	**scream**	**demolish**

- Linking verbs:

  include any "to be" verb and any verb that can logically be replaced by a "to be" verb

  She **seems** nice. — She **is** nice.
  The flower **smells** stinky. — The flower **is** stinky.

  Seems and *smells* are linking verbs.

EXERCISE 26: IDENTIFYING VERBS: Circle the verbs in the following sentences.

1. The night is always darkest before the dawn.
2. Nothing tastes better than a grilled cheese sandwich.
3. Emily admired Katniss, so she decided to take archery lessons.
4. The dog howled as he chased the cat around the yard.

EXERCISE 27: IDENTIFYING VERBS IN CONTEXT: Underline each verb in the following sentences.

Everything seemed strange when they went down. Hannah's familiar face looked unnatural as she flew about the kitchen. The big trunk stood ready in the hall, and Mother's cloak and bonnet lay on the sofa. Nobody talked much, but as the time drew near, Mrs. March said to the girls, "Children, I leave you to Hannah's care. I have no fears for you. Go on with your work as usual, for work is a blessed solace."

- **SENTENCE WRITING PRACTICE 9:** On the lines below, compose five sentences, each containing action verbs.

1. ____

____

2. ____

____

3. ____

____

4. ____

____

5. ____

____

VERB PHRASES

A verb often consists of two or more words:

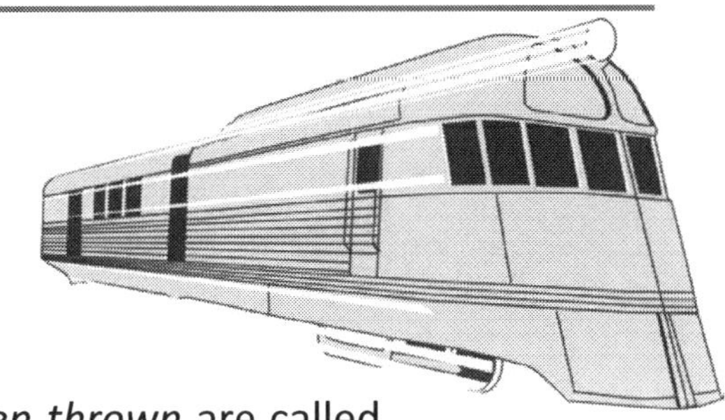

I *have ridden* the train before.
The people *were rushing* by.
Henry *has* never *been* on a train.

In these sentences, *have learned, were rushing*, and *has been thrown* are called verb phrases. A **verb phrase** is a group of two or more words used as one verb: **My brother *has come*.**

The parts of a verb-phrase may be separated by other words:

The train *will* soon *arrive*.
I *have* often *seen* your cousin.

The forms of the verb *be* are often used in verb phrases and are then called auxiliary verbs. Auxiliary means helping. English has three auxiliary verbs: *be, have,* and *do.* Each of these verbs can be used as a regular verb as well.

am, are, is, was, were, be, being, been
have, has, had
do, does, did

Another set of verbs, known as **modal verbs**, can stand alone or act together with other verbs. They do not get conjugated with subject or tense, and do not ever change form. There is no present or past participle for these verbs. When they act together with other verbs, they behave like auxiliary verbs. English modal verbs are:

may, might, must
shall, should
can, could
will, would, ought

EXERCISE 28: IDENTIFYING VERB PHRASES: Underline the verb phrases in these sentences.

1. The children were playing on the seashore.
2. I will now write a letter.
3. I do not like his looks.
4. Do you hear your father?
5. Lost time is never found again.
6. Have you ever read *Robinson Crusoe*?
7. When does your birthday come?

- **SENTENCE WRITING PRACTICE 10:** When writing, students sometimes use too many verb phrases, making their writing sound weak. Rewrite the following sentences. Remove the verb phrases and replace them with action verbs. See the first example.

1. Coming-of-age ceremonies are still performed by many communities.

Many communities still perform coming of age ceremonies.

2. Dame Van Winkle was always keeping her house in neat order.

3. My dog has forgotten me!

4. Brightly the sunset was lighting the village street.

5. Reports of the value of his invention were rapidly circulated by the people.

6. The curfew bell was ringing loudly.

7. He was whirling his lasso with an easy turn of his wrist.

8. The rain was tapping softly at my door.

9. The baby was sleeping until she entered the room.

10. Mowgli was rounding up a buffalo herd at the head of the ravine.

VERB TENSES

The tense of a verb gives an indication of time. There are three basic or **simple tenses**: past, present, and future.

- The **present tense** represents action in the present.
  I **am.** They **go** now**.**

- The **past tense** represents action in the past.
  They **ran.** We **were calling** yesterday**.**

- The **future tense** represents action in the future.
  I **shall go.** They **will call** tomorrow**.**

EXERCISE 29: Underline the verb(s) in each sentence. On the line provided, write whether the verb is in the past, present, or future tense.

1. Who fed the Robin? ____________________
2. We will expect you at noon. ____________________
3. No mate, no comrade, Lucy knew. ____________________
4. They are fighting for the cause of justice. ____________________
5. They will fight for the cause of justice. ____________________
6. They fought for the cause of justice. ____________________
7. Father says no one will ever know why the ship sank. ____________________

____

____

EXERCISE 30: Rewrite the following sentences, changing the verbs to the present tense.

1. The brook splashed and murmured down the glen.

____

____

2. The boys will fish in it all morning.

____

____

REGULAR AND IRREGULAR VERBS

The key to using the correct verb tense is knowing the verb's present tense, past tense, and past participle. Every other part of a verb is formed from one of these.

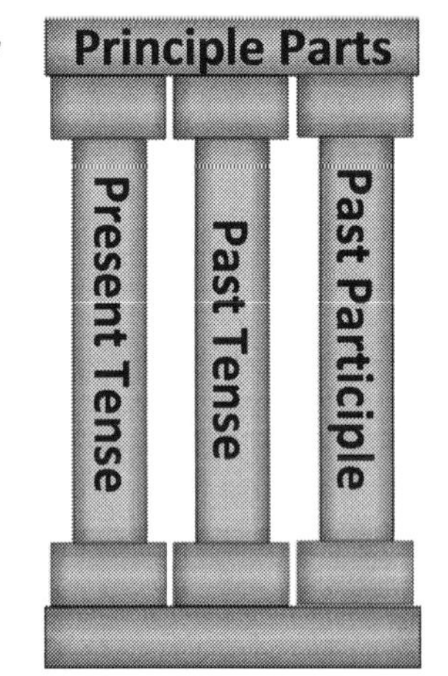

The present tense, the past tense, and the past participle are called the **principal parts** of a verb.

To identify the principal parts of a verb, we use the following template:

I _____ now.	I **hope** now.	Present Tense
I __________ yesterday.	I **hoped** yesterday.	Past Tense
I have _____________.	I have **hoped**.	Past Participle

Notice how the verbs in these sentences form the past tense and the past participle:

Present:	I help now.	I **help** you.
Past:	I helped yesterday.	I **helped** you.
Past Participle:	I have helped.	I have **helped** you.
Present:	I see now.	We **see** them.
Past:	I saw yesterday.	We **saw** them.
Past Participle:	I have seen.	We have **seen** them.
Present:	I live now.	They **live** well.
Past:	I lived yesterday.	They **lived** well.
Past Participle:	I have lived.	They have **lived** well.

Most English verbs form their past tense and past participle by adding *ed*, *d*, or *t* to the present tense.

- A verb that forms its past tense and past participle by adding *ed, d*, or *t* to the present tense is called a **regular verb**.
- A verb that forms its past tense and past participle in some other way is called an **irregular verb.**

Help is a regular verb. *See* is an irregular verb. (See above.) *Give* is also an example of an irregular verb.

Present:	They **give** liberally.
Past:	They **gave** liberally.
Past Participle:	They have **given** liberally.

PRINCIPAL PARTS

Many grammatical mistakes are made from not knowing the principal parts of verbs. The principal parts include the **simple, past,** and **past participle** forms. The first two forms you already know. The third, the past participle, is the verb form used with auxiliary verbs *be* and *have*. Learn the table below.

PRESENT	PAST	PAST PARTICIPLE
beat	beat	beaten
begin	began	begun
bet	bet	bet
bite	bit	bitten
blow	blew	blown
break	broke	broken
bring	brought	brought
build	built	built
burst	burst	burst
buy	bought	bought
catch	caught	caught
choose	chose	chosen
cling	clung	clung
come	came	come
creep	crept	crept
dive	dove	dived
do	did	done
draw	drew	drawn
eat	ate	eaten
fall	fell	fallen
feel	felt	felt
fight	fought	fought
flee	fled	fled
fly	flew	flown
flow	flowed	flowed
forsake	forsook	forsaken
freeze	froze	frozen
get	got	got
give	gave	given
go	went	gone
grow	grew	grown
hide	hid	hidden

PRESENT	PAST	PAST PARTICIPLE
hurt	hurt	hurt
know	knew	known
lay	laid	laid
lie (recline)	lay	lain
lie (fib)	lied	lied
raise	raised	raised
ride	rode	ridden
ring	rang	rung
rise	rose	risen
run	ran	run
see	saw	seen
set	set	set
shake	shook	shaken
shine	shone	shone
show	showed	shown
shrink	shrank	shrunk
sing	sang	sung
sink	sank	sunk
sit	sat	sat
slay	slew	slain
sling	slung	slung
speak	spoke	spoken
spend	spent	spent
spring	sprang	sprung
steal	stole	stolen
stick	stuck	stuck
sting	stung	stung
strike	struck	struck
string	strung	strung
strive	strove	striven
swear	swore	sworn
swell	swelled	swollen
swim	swam	swum
swing	swung	swung
take	took	taken
teach	taught	taught
tear	tore	torn
throw	threw	thrown
thrust	thrust	thrust
tread	trod	trodden

PRESENT	PAST	PAST PARTICIPLE
wear	wore	worn
weave	wove	woven
weep	wept	wept
wet	wet	wet
win	won	won
wind	wound	wound
wring	wrung	wrung
write	wrote	written

EXERCISE 31: Study and memorize the principal parts for the verbs in the previously given table. When you are ready, complete the table below.

PRESENT	PAST	PAST PARTICIPLE
beat		
begin		
bet		
bite		
blow		
break		
bring		
build		
burst		
buy		
catch		
choose		
cling		
come		
creep		
dive		
do		
draw		
eat		
fall		
feel		
fight		
flee		
fly		
flow		
forsake		

PRESENT	PAST	PAST PARTICIPLE
freeze		
get		
give		
go		
grow		
hide		
hurt		
know		
lay		
lie (recline)		
lie (fib)		
raise		
ride		
ring		
rise		
run		
see		
set		
shake		
shine		
show		
shrink		
sing		
sink		
sit		
slay		
sling		

PRESENT	PAST	PAST PARTICIPLE
speak		
spend		
spring		
steal		
stick		
sting		
strike		
string		
strive		
swear		
swell		
swim		
swing		
take		
teach		
tear		
throw		
thrust		
tread		
wear		
weave		
weep		
wet		
win		
wind		
wring		
write		

HAVE, HAS, HAD: AUXILIARY

We often wish to express an action as occurring in time in relation to another action. For example, we may wish to express that the present is heavily influenced by the recent past, or discuss two events occurring in relation to one another at two different points in the past or in the future.

To express an action as having a time relationship with another action in the past, present, or future, we use a verb phrase consisting of a form of the appropriate form of the verb *have* and the past participle of the verb representing the action.

- The form of a verb that denotes action began in the past but completed in the present is called the **present perfect aspect.** (Also denotes action began in the past but is ongoing in the present or may occur again.)

There! I have written my assignment.	Began in the past / completed in the present
He has not finished his assignment yet.	Began in the past / not finished, ongoing

- The form of a verb that denotes that an action has been completed in the past before some other time in the past is called the **past perfect aspect.**

Yesterday, when school ended, I had written two pages.

Completed in the past (written two pages) before some other time in the past (when school ended).

- The form of a verb that denotes that an action will have been completed at some point in the future is called the **future perfect aspect.**

Friday, when school begins, I will have written a new story.

Completed at some point in the future (will have written a new story), before some other point in the future (when school begins).

ASPECTS OF THE VERB "to be" FOR THE PRONOUN (I)

Simple Aspects:	
Present:	I **am**
Past	I **was**
Future:	I will **be**
Perfect Aspects:	
Present Perfect:	I have **been**
Past Perfect:	I had **been**
Future Perfect:	I will have **been**

On the following page, you can find the three simple and three perfect aspects of the verb "*to see*."

Present Simple	I see	You see	He sees She sees It sees	We see	You see	They see
Past Simple	I saw	You saw	He saw She saw It saw	We saw	You saw	They saw
Future Simple	I will see	You will see	He will see She will see It will see	We will see	You will see	They will see
Present Perfect	I have seen	You have seen	He has seen She has seen It has seen	We have seen	You have seen	They have seen
Past Perfect	I had seen	You had seen	He had seen She had seen It had seen	We had seen	You had seen	They had seen
Future Perfect	I will have seen	You will have seen	He will have seen She will have seen It will have seen	We will have seen	You will have seen	They will have seen

ASPECTS OF THE VERB "WRITE"

Simple Aspects:
Present: I **write**
Past: I **wrote**
Future: I will **write**
Perfect Aspects:
Present Perfect: I have **written**
Past Perfect: I had **written**
Future Perfect: I will have **written**

EXERCISE 32: For the pronoun I, conjugate the aspects of the following verbs: call, run, sleep, and play.

ASPECTS OF THE VERB "call"

Simple Aspects:
Present: I ____________________

Past: I ____________________

Future: I ____________________

Perfect Aspects:
Present Perfect: I have ____________________

Past Perfect: I had ____________________

Future Perfect: I will have ____________________

ASPECTS OF THE VERB "run"

Simple Aspects:
Present: I ____________________

Past: I ____________________

Future: I ____________________

Perfect Aspects:
Present Perfect: I ____________________

Past Perfect: I ____________________

Future Perfect: I ____________________

ASPECTS OF THE VERB "sleep"

Simple Aspects:

Present: I ________________________

Past: I ________________________

Future: I ________________________

Perfect Aspects:

Present Perfect: I ________________________

Past Perfect: I ________________________

Future Perfect: I ________________________

ASPECTS OF THE VERB "play"

Simple Aspects:

Present: I ________________________

Past: I ________________________

Future: I ________________________

Perfect Aspects:

Present Perfect: I ________________________

Past Perfect: I ________________________

Future Perfect: I ________________________

Exercise 33: On the line provided, write the aspect of each verb in the following sentences. (For help, refer to the table on page 42. To help you determine the aspect, replace the subject with a pronoun.)

1. Katharine (*she*) *has* just *read* that book. ________________________
2. John will have finished it in an hour. ________________________
3. He had nearly finished it before supper time. ________________________
4. Where have you been all these years? ________________________
5. I hope you will call often, now that you have returned. ________________________

   ____

6. Many inventors had attempted flying machines before the Wrights built their successful airplane. ________________________

   ____

PROGRESSIVE ASPECTS AND EMPHATIC FORMS

We often use a form of the verb *is* and a present participle to represent an action as progressing or continuing: **I am writing.**

A verb phrase consisting of a form of the verb *be* and a present participle (-ing form) is said to be in the **progressive aspect**. It is also referred to as the **continuous aspect**.

There are six progressive aspects. They are formed from the three simple aspects (present, past, and future) and the three perfect aspects (present perfect, past perfect, and future perfect).

The progressive aspects of *see* are:

Present Progressive:	I **am seeing**	You **are seeing**	He/she/it **is seeing**
Present Progressive:	We **are seeing**	You **are seeing**	They **are seeing**
Past Progressive:	I **was seeing**	You **were seeing**	He/she/it **was seeing**
Past Progressive:	We **were seeing**	You **were seeing**	They **were seeing**
Future Progressive:	I **will be seeing**	You **will be seeing**	He/she/it **will be seeing**
Future Progressive:	We **will be seeing**	You **will be seeing**	They **will be seeing**
Present Perfect Prog:	I **have been seeing**	You **have been seeing**	He/she/it **has been seeing**
Present Perfect Prog:	We **have been seeing**	You **have been seeing**	They **have been seeing**
Past Perfect Prog:	I **had been seeing**	You **had been seeing**	He/she/it **had been seeing**
Past Perfect Prog:	We **had been seeing**	You **had been seeing**	They **had been seeing**
Future Perfect Prog:	I **will have been seeing**	You **will have been seeing**	He/she/it **will have been seeing**
Future Perfect Prog:	We **will have been seeing**	You **will have been seeing**	They **will have been seeing**

To add emphasis, we use the **emphatic form**. The emphatic form is created by adding *do*, *does*, or *did* to the simple present of a verb.

The emphatic forms of *write* are:

Present Emphatic:	I **do** write.	You **do** write.	(He, she, it) **does** write.
	We **do** write.	You **do** write.	They **do** write.
Past Emphatic:	I **did** write.	You **did** write.	(He, she, it) **did** write.
	We **did** write.	You **did** write.	They **did** write.

These same verb phrases are also used in interrogative sentences by inverting the order of the subject and the verb. They are also used with the adverb *not* to create negative sentences.

Present Interrogative:	**Do** you **write**?	**Does** he **write**?	**Do** they **write**?
Present Negative:	I **do** not **write**.	He **does** not **write**.	They **do** not **write**.

EXERCISE 34: Conjugate the six progressive aspects of call, speak, and work.

PROGRESSIVE ASPECTS OF THE VERB "WRITE"

Present Progressive: I am ______________________
Past Progressive: I was ______________________
Future Progressive: I will be ______________________

Present Perfect Progressive: I have been ______________________
Past Perfect Progressive: I had been ______________________
Future Perfect Progressive: I will have been ______________________

PROGRESSIVE ASPECTS OF THE VERB "SPEAK"

Present Progressive: I am ______________________
Past Progressive: I was ______________________
Future Progressive: I will be ______________________

Present Perfect Progressive: I have been ______________________
Past Perfect Progressive: I had been ______________________
Future Perfect Progressive: I will have been ______________________

PROGRESSIVE ASPECTS OF THE VERB "WORK"

Present Progressive: I ______________________
Past Progressive: I ______________________
Future Progressive: I ______________________

Present Perfect Progressive: I ______________________
Past Perfect Progressive: I ______________________
Future Perfect Progressive: I ______________________

EXERCISE 35: Write six sentences—the first three using the present emphatic form of the given verb and the other three using the past emphatic form of the given verb. Create the present emphatic by using the words *do* or *does*. Create the past emphatic by using the word *did*.

1. write ____

2. speak ____

3. work ____

4. write ____

5. speak ____

6. work ____

EXERCISE 36: Underline the verbs in the following sentences. Write the tense/aspect/form of each verb on the lines provided. (For help, refer to page 45. Hint: Replace the subject with a pronoun.)

1. Mildred has been boating all morning. (Ex: She has been boating...)

____

2. Do you enjoy boating?

____

3. No, I do not enjoy it.

____

4. I did enjoy it before our boating accident.

____

5. Mildred and Elizabeth are reading now; they will be eating lunch soon.

____

____

SOME TROUBLESOME VERBS

In the passages below, *saw* and *seen* are used correctly.

Tip **saw** many strange sights in the city that day. When he returned to the Home, the kind Doctor asked him what he had **seen**.

"O Doctor, I have **seen** such wonderful sights! They can't be real!"

"Hmmm," said the Doctor. "I believe the boy thinks he has **seen** Wonderland!"

Here are more examples of the perfect aspect.

I **saw** the bird. The boy **has seen** it also. (Both saw the bird, but at different times.)

We **went** to see John. John **had gone** to school. (John had already left.)

Stacie **ate** all of her food. Soon Jim **will have eaten** all of his, too. (In the future.)

EXERCISE 37: As you can see, the sentences below contain missing verbs. Complete the sentence by adding the verb form indicated. If needed, refer to pages 41 and 42 for assistance.

Past	Present Perfect	Past Perfect	Future Perfect
An oak **grew** at the gate.	It <u>has grown</u> for years.	It <u>had grown</u> for years.	It <u>will have grown</u> for years.
Tom **knew** the secret.	He ________________ it for a week.	He ________________ it for a week.	He ________________ it for a week.
The boys **threw** the ball.	They ________________ it often.	They ________________ it often.	They ________________ it often.
You **ate** the cake.	You ________________ every crumb	You ________________ every crumb	You ________________ every crumb
Fido **bit** the man.	He ________________ many people.	He ________________ many people.	He ________________ many people.

LIE, LAY

There are two little verbs that are often misused. They are *lie* and *lay*.

Lie means to recline. *Lay* means to place in position. Sometimes, however, *lay* is used as the past tense of *lie*.

"Laid, on the other hand, always means placed. "

I *lay* the book on the table, and the book *lies* there still.

The verb **lay** is followed by an object. I **lay** the *book* on the table. *Book* is the object. The verb **lie** means to rest and does not need an object. The book **lies** there.

You will get a better idea of the correct use of these words by studying the following sentences:

No Object:	**I *lie* in the sand.**	**I *lay* in the sand.**	**I *have lain* in the sand.**
	I *lie*.	**I *lay*.**	**I *have lain*.**
Object:	**I *lay* the book down.**	**I *laid* the book there.**	**I *have laid* it there.**

EXERCISE 38: Use the proper form of lie or lay in the sentences.

1. I frequently ____________________ on the grass.
2. I have ____________________ under that tree many times.
3. I have ____________________ the book on the table.
4. Yesterday, the book ____________________ on the table.
5. Chickens ____________________ eggs.
6. That particular chicken has ____________________ several eggs today.
7. He has ____________________ his hat on the counter.
8. The book ____________________ on the table now.
9. The book has ____________________ on the table for a long time.
10. Please, ____________________ the book down.

SIT, SET

Sit and *set* are two other little words that trouble many people. Sometimes **set** means to cause to sit. *Sit* means to take a seat. *Set* means to place.

The verb **set** is followed by an object. *Book* is the object.

I *set* the book down.

The verb **sit** means to rest in a seat and does not need an object.

The cat *sat* there.

You will get a better idea of the correct use of these words by studying the following sentences:

	I *sit* in the chair.	**I *sit*.**
No Object:	**I *sat* in the chair.**	**I *sat.***
	I have *sat* in the chair.	**I have *sat*.**
	I *set* the pitcher down.	
Object:	**I *set* the pitcher down yesterday.**	
	I have *set* the pitcher down.	

EXERCISE 39: Use the correct form of set or sit in the sentence.

1. The boy was _______________ to work.
2. The sun _______________ in the west.
3. Have you _______________ the supper table?
4. The doctor _______________ the broken bone.
5. We _______________ out early in the morning.
6. Do you _______________ a good example?
7. The ring was _______________ with jewels.
8. _______________ in this chair.
9. The bird _______________ on her eggs.
10. The bird has _______________ on her eggs.

TRANSITIVE AND INTRANSITIVE VERBS

There are five basic sentence patterns in the English language. These patterns all include a subject and a predicate, but the specific kinds of subjects, verbs, extra nouns, pronouns, or adjectives determine the pattern of the sentence.

Before we can understand each sentence pattern, we need to learn about transitive and intransitive verbs.

Some verbs are complete in themselves, and some require objects in order to make a complete statement or assertion. In sentences such as *The sun shines* or *The clock ticks*, the verb by itself makes a complete statement about the subject. These are **intransitive verbs**. Intransitive verbs do not need an object to assert a statement about the subject.

His hand *trembles*.
The light *disappeared*.
The cat *ran*.

In sentences such as *The farmer planted trees* or *Fred threw the ball*, the verb alone does not make a complete statement about the subject. Another word, an object, is needed to show what receives the action of the verb. These are **transitive verbs**. Transitive verbs need direct objects to make a complete statement about the subject.

If we heard a person say *Charles found*, we would naturally ask *Found what*?

I *invited* him.
Charles *found* the key.
The cat *caught* the mouse.

Verbs like *catch* and *invite*, which require an object to show the person or thing that receives the action, are called **transitive verbs**. The word that shows the person or thing receiving the action is usually a noun or pronoun. It is called the **direct object**. The words *him*, *key*, and *mouse* are direct objects.

- A **transitive verb** is a verb that has a direct object.

Robbers *attacked* the bank. Bank is the direct object.

- An **intransitive verb** is a verb that does not have a direct object.

The wind *blows*.

To find the object of a transitive verb, ask questions such as *Catch what? Invited whom?*

Many verbs can be either transitive or intransitive. The underlined words below are direct objects.

TRANSITIVE	**INTRANSITIVE**
We *break* the ice.	**The waves *break* on the shore.**
He *moves* the table.	**The train *moves* slowly.**
He *slammed* the door.	**The door *slammed*.**
The sun *melts* the snow.	**The snow *melts*.**
He *boils* the water.	**The water *boils*.**

EXERCISE 40: TRANSITIVE VS INTRANSITIVE VERBS: Tell whether each verb in these sentences is transitive or intransitive. Write transitive or intransitive on the lines provided. If the verb is transitive, underline its object.

1. The troops retired slowly. ______________________________

2. Contractors build houses. ______________________________

3. I looked down from my window. ______________________________

4. Matthew Henson explored the arctic. ______________________________

5. Benjamin Franklin invented stoves. ______________________________

6. The athletes jumped over the fence. ______________________________

EXERCISE 41: For each of the paragraphs below, underline each noun once and each verb twice.

Once upon a time the king of a large and rich country gathered together his army to take a faraway little country. The king and his soldiers marched all morning long then camped in the forest.

"Don't go today," said his landlord; "my wife bakes tomorrow, and she shall make you a cake."

Ivan headed for the door.

"Here," said the landlord, "here is a cake for you and your wife; and when you are most joyous together, then break the cake, but not sooner."

ACTIVE AND PASSIVE VERBS

Compare the following sentences:

1. My uncle painted this house. **(active)**
2. This house was painted by my uncle. **(passive="to be" + past participle of the verb)**

In both sentences, the word *uncle* is the **doer** of the action, and the word *house* is the **receiver** of the action, or the object of the verb.

When the doer is the subject, the sentence is said to have the **active voice**. When the object or receiver is the subject of the sentence, the sentence is said to have the **passive voice**. To include the doer of the action in a passive sentence, the doer goes in a *by* phrase after the verb.

EXERCISE 42: Write whether each sentence is active or passive. If the sentence is passive, rewrite the sentence in the active voice. If the sentence is active, rewrite the sentence in passive voice.

1. The animals were fed by the farmer. ____________________

____

____

2. The farmers opened the flood gates. ____________________

____

____

3. Mr. Long's house was destroyed by fire. ____________________

____

____

4. All grocers sell flour, tea, and coffee. ____________________

____

____

5. Ichabod heard the barking of the watchdog. ____________________

____

____

- **SENTENCE WRITING PRACTICE 11:** On the lines provided, imitate the sentences below by composing five pairs of sentences that say the same thing; make one active voice and one passive voice. Notice how the object of the active voice sentence becomes the subject of the passive voice sentence.

Virtue **ennobles** the mind. The mind **is ennobled** by virtue.

William **conquered** Harold. Harold **was conquered** by William.

The tree **was struck** by lightning. Lightning **struck** the tree.

1. ______________________________

____

____

2. ______________________________

____

____

3. ______________________________

____

____

4. ______________________________

____

____

5. ______________________________

____

____

PRONOUNS

In the following sentences, notice which words refer to birds and thread without naming either.

Some birds sew leaves together for their nests. They use thread, which they themselves make from cotton. They use their bills for needles.

The word *they* is used in place of the noun *birds* and prevents the author from repeating the word *birds* over and over. Also, the word *which* is used in place of the noun *thread*. Such words are called **pronouns**.

A **pronoun** is a word used instead of a noun. If we had no pronouns, we could not avoid awkward repetitions like these:

John thought John had lost John's money.

By using pronouns, we can say:

John thought he had lost his money.

Some important pronouns are:

Personal Pronouns	Possessive Pronouns	Relative Pronouns	Demonstrative Pronouns	Interrogative Pronouns
I, you, he, she, it, we, you, they, me, him, her, us, them	mine, yours, his, hers, its, ours, theirs	who, whom, whoever, whomever, what, whose, whatever, whichever, that, which	this, that, these, those	who, whom, what, which, whose

When writing with pronouns, you must first use the noun to tell the reader which word the pronoun is replacing. This noun is called the antecedent. The **antecedent** of a pronoun is the word or words for which the pronoun stands.

She lost her ring — Who is she? There is no antecedent.
Emma lost her ring. — Emma is the antecedent.

EXERCISE 43: Rewrite the following sentences using pronouns in place of nouns wherever you can. On your sentences, underline the antecedent.

1. Boone lived alone until Boone's brother returned.

2. Seals are killed when seals are about four years old.

3. The hunter soon saw the hunter's mistake.

4. Franklin and Franklin's playmates used to fish for minnows in a mill pond.

5. I have not seen John and Charles since I met John and Charles at your house.

6. The birds use thread, thread the birds themselves make from cotton.

7. Benedict Arnold, Benedict Arnold was accused of treason, is infamous.

PERSONAL PRONOUNS

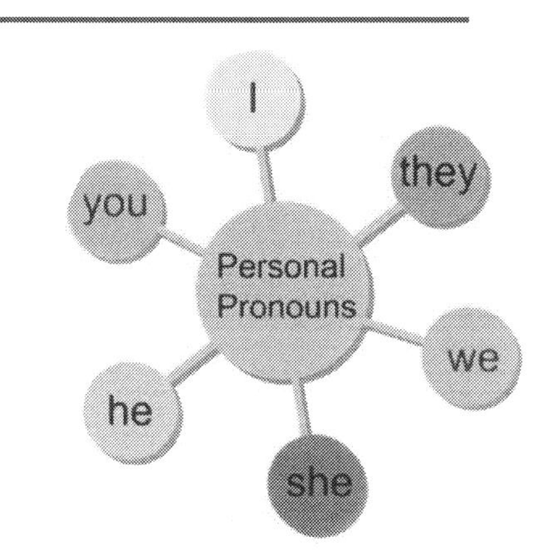

A pronoun that shows by its form whether it stands for the person speaking, the person spoken to, or the person spoken of is called a **personal pronoun**.

Pronouns that stand for the person speaking are called
first person pronouns.
Pronouns that stand for the person spoken to are called
second person pronouns.
Pronouns that stand for the person spoken about are called
third person pronouns.

	Singular	Plural	Possessive
First Person	I, me	we, us, our, ours	my, mine, our, ours,
Second Person	you	you	your, yours
Third Person	he, him, she, her, it	they, them, their, theirs	his, her, hers, its, their, theirs

Many people make mistakes in using personal pronouns. They often use **subject pronouns** as objects and **object pronouns** as subjects.

Subject Pronouns		Object Pronouns	
Singular	Plural	Singular	Plural
I	we	me	us
you	you	you	you
he, she, it	they	him, her, it	them

Subject pronouns are used as subjects and after forms of the verb "to be."

***We* went to the store.**	Subject
The person on the phone was *she*.	Subject pronouns follow linking verbs.
It is *I*.	

Object pronouns are properly used as objects: direct objects, indirect objects, and objects of the preposition.

Recall that **direct objects** are the nouns required by and following transitive verbs. The sentence doesn't make sense without the object. Whether or not a direct object is required depends on the verb.

An **indirect object** is not required by the verb, and the words can be moved around so that the indirect object falls within a prepositional phrase. In this case, the object of the preposition is also the indirect object of the sentence.

Joseph put *it* on the table. — *It* is the direct object.
Tell *her* the truth. (or Tell the truth to *her*.) — *Her* is the indirect object.
For *me*, reading is rather fun. — *Me* is the object of the preposition.

Two words may be used together as the subject of a sentence.

Jason and I *were* late. — *Jason* and *I* form a compound subject.
We *were* late. — (Note: The compound subject uses the plural verb.)

Likewise, two words may be the object of one verb or the object of the preposition.

Father praised *him* and *me*. — *Him* and *me* form a compound direct object.
I sat between *him* and *Tom*. — *Him* and *Tom* form a compound object of the preposition.

EXERCISE 44: In the following exercise, choose the correct pronoun for the sentence. For sentences 16 to 20, choose an appropriate pronoun.

1. He and (I, me) met at the gymnasium.
2. Her mother and (she, her) set out yesterday.
3. Did the teacher refer to you or (I, me)?
4. (We, us) boys are planning a sleigh ride.
5. (She, her) and Jane refused to go.
6. Luke was standing between John and (he, him).
7. (They, them) are the men we saw on the bridge.
8. (They, them) and (we, us) then hurried away.
9. (He, him) and (I, me) were feeding the squirrels.
10. Between you and (I, me), Richard is mistaken.
11. He gave it to Sophie and ________________. (I, me)
12. The teacher and ________________ modeled that map. (I, me)
13. Louis and ________________ have saved a dollar. (I, me)
14. Caroline or ________________ must stay at home. (I, me)
15. Did you call mother or ________________? (I, me)
16. When the man passed, the dogs barked at ________________.
17. Arthur whistled for ________________ dog, but ________________ did not come.
18. The schoolhouse had a large tree in front of ________________.
19. If James wants the book, let ________________ have ________________.
20. The teacher asked ________________ students to prepare ________________ lessons.

ADJECTIVES, ARTICLES

We have found that everything has a name and that every name is a **noun;** however, things may have the same name but be different.

In the sentence *George owns a dog*, the name *dog* does not show what kind of dog George has. It may be large or small, black or white, gentle or savage, good or bad.

A word used with a noun to make the meaning more definite is called an **adjective**. The word adjective means added to. **Adjectives** are words that modify or describe nouns.

beautiful   grey   five
that   the teacher's   only

Imagine there are five backpacks on a table. You need to tell your friend which backpack(s) to grab. Adjectives would help as you tell her:

The smallest backpack	which
My backpack	whose
The canvas backpack	what kind
The two backpacks on the left	how many

- A **Descriptive Adjective** may describe by showing what kind.

pure water   **sweet water**

- A **Limiting Adjective** may limit by showing which one, how much, or how many

this book   **much money**
six apples   **last dime**

- An adjective may also be formed from nouns and pronouns. Adjectives formed from Proper Nouns are called **Proper Adjectives.**

winter sports	**English sports**	**that sport**
sea monster	**Loch Ness Monster**	**his monster**

- *This*, *that*, *these*, and *those* are called **Demonstrative Adjectives.**

- Adjectives formed from pronouns that show possession are called **Possessive Adjectives.**

This is *our* car.	Possessive Adjectives (followed by a noun) (my, your, his, her, its, our, their)
That car is *ours*.	Possessive Pronouns (replaces the noun) (mine, yours, his, hers, its, ours, theirs)

- An adjective may be formed from **Interrogative Pronouns**

which **car** ***whose*** **shoes** ***what*** **school**

ARTICLES

There are only three articles—*a, an*, and *the*.

The **horse is ready.**

The words *a, an*, and *the* work like **adjectives** because they modify the meaning of nouns, but they are called **articles**. They are also known as **noun markers** because they are always followed by nouns.

The is called the **definite article** because it is used to point out one or more definite nouns.

The **front door** ***The*** **boys on** ***the*** **back seats**

A and *an* are called **indefinite articles** because they are used to point to any one of a kind of noun.

An **orange is round.** ***A*** **room on the third floor**

The form *an* is used before words beginning with a vowel sound (a, e, i, o, u) or silent h—as in *an* oak or *an* honest man. In other positions, the form *a* is used—*a* star, *a* year, or *a* world.

EXERCISE 45: IDENTIFYING ADJECTIVES: Circle the adjectives in the following sentences. Underline the nouns they describe. Place a square around the articles.

1. The yellow flower glistened in the hot summer sun.
2. The hungry dog barked for his dinner.
3. Marley's seven brothers grumbled when she asked to watch her favorite princess movie.
4. Without warning, the hot flames turned the wooden door into ashes.
5. A majority of middle school students believed that the math final should be cancelled.

EXERCISE 46: In the following sentences, underline each adjective. On the blank line, write **descriptive, demonstrative, limiting, proper, or possessive.** (Refer to pages 59 and 60 if needed.)

Ex.: <u>Many</u> <u>rich</u> men live in <u>large</u> houses. limiting
descriptive
descriptive

1. The clever burglar entered by the back door. ____________ ____________

2. The blue book belongs on the white shelf. ____________ ____________

3. Turn to the forty-third page. ____________

4. My new school has sixteen rooms. ____________ ____________ ____________

5. The sailors escaped in two small boats. ____________ ____________

6. The twelve jurors spent six weeks deliberating. ____________ ____________

7. That American flag is his flag. ____________ ____________ ____________

8. The English knights fought to the death. ____________

COMPARATIVE ADJECTIVES

Read the following sentences.

1. **Fred is a *tall* boy.**
2. **George is *taller* than Fred.**
3. **Francine is the *tallest* student.**

In sentence 1, the adjective *tall* modifies boy. In sentence 2, George is compared with Fred by changing the form of the adjective to *taller*. In sentence 3, Francine is compared with all the other students in school by changing the form to *tallest*.

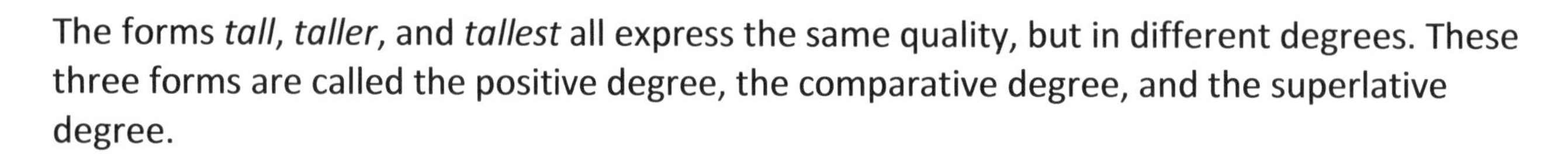

The forms *tall*, *taller*, and *tallest* all express the same quality, but in different degrees. These three forms are called the positive degree, the comparative degree, and the superlative degree.

- The **positive degree** is used when no direct comparison is made. It expresses the simple quality.

  This is a large tree.

- The **comparative degree** is used when one object or class is compared with another. It expresses a higher (or lower) degree of the quality. Often the word *than* follows the comparative degree.

  This tree is larger *than* that.
  Maples are smaller *than* Elms.

- The **superlative degree** is used when one object or class is compared with two or more other objects. It expresses the highest (or lowest) degree of the quality.

  This is the largest tree in the grove.
  This is the smallest tree.

Notice the following changes in spelling when the endings *er* and *est* are added.

- If the positive degree ends in *e*, the *e* is dropped:

brave	braver	bravest
handsome	handsomer	handsomest
feeble	feebler	feeblest

- If the positive degree ends in *y*, preceded by a consonant, the *y* is changed to *i*:

happy	happier	happiest
merry	merrier	merriest
dry	drier	driest

- If the positive degree is a one syllable adjective, ending in a consonant preceded by a single vowel, double the consonant:

sad	sadder	saddest
hot	hotter	hottest
slim	slimmer	slimmest
flat	flatter	flattest

- If the adjective with two syllables sounds awkward with the use of *–er* and *–est*, use *more* and *most* (or *less* and *least*).

heavy	heavier	heaviest
famous	more famous	most famous
handsome	more handsome	most handsome

Comparison by means of *er* and *est* is called **regular comparison**. Comparison by means of *more* and *most* (or *less* and *least*) is called **adverbial comparison**.

- If the adjective has three or more syllables, use *more* and *most* (or *less* and *least*).

terrible	more terrible	most terrible

Mary is an *attentive* pupil.
Mary is *more attentive* than her sister.
Mary is the *most attentive* pupil in the class.

- Some adjectives are irregular in their comparison. In some instances the comparative and superlative are borrowed from other adjectives.

good	better	best
little	less	least
much	more	most

- Some adjectives denote qualities which by their nature cannot vary in degree.

right	wrong	triangular
daily	annual	eternal
infinite	occasional	solar
three	five	second

all proper adjectives

EXERCISE 47: Study the table of adjectives that follows. When you are ready, proceed to the following page and complete the table, adding the comparative and superlative.

Adjective	Comparative	Superlative
bad	worse	worst
big	bigger	biggest
boring	more boring	most boring
busy	busier	busiest
comfortable	more comfortable	most comfortable
cute	cuter	cutest
dirty	dirtier	dirtiest
dishonest	more dishonest	most dishonest
dry	drier (dryer)	driest (driest)
early	earlier	earliest
easy	easier	easiest
expensive	more expensive	most expensive
famous	more famous	most famous
fast	faster	fastest
friendly	friendlier	friendliest
generous	more generous	most generous
gloomy	gloomier	gloomiest
good	better	best
healthy	healthier	healthiest
high	higher	highest
honest	more honest	most honest
hot	hotter	hottest
interesting	more interesting	most interesting
kind	kinder	kindest
large	larger	largest
little	less	least
long	longer	longest
many	more	most
much	more	most
nice	nicer	nicest
pretty	prettier	prettiest
quiet	quieter	quietest
sad	sadder	saddest
safe	safer	safest
short	shorter	shortest
terrific	more terrific	most terrific
wise	wiser	wisest
young	younger	youngest

Adjective	Comparative	Superlative
bad		
big		
boring		
busy		
comfortable		
cute		
dirty		
dishonest		
dry		
early		
easy		
expensive		
famous		
fast		
friendly		
generous		
gloomy		
good		
healthy		
high		
honest		
hot		
interesting		
kind		
large		
little		
long		
many		
much		
nice		
pretty		
quiet		
sad		
safe		
short		
terrific		
wise		
young		

- **SENTENCE WRITING PRACTICE 12**: For each of the adjectives below, write three sentences. One using the positive degree, one the comparative degree, and one the superlative degree.

1. Fred is a **tall** boy.
2. George is a **taller** boy *than* Fred.
3. Frank is the **tallest** boy in school.

1. quiet

____

____

____

____

____

2. terrific

____

____

____

____

____

3. healthy

____

____

____

____

____

4. wise

____

____

____

____

____

ADVERBS

Adverbs are words that modify verbs, adjectives, or other adverbs. Just as an adjective is often used to modify a noun, we use adverbs to modify verbs. Most verbs express action. This action may vary as to manner, time, place, or other circumstances.

A word that is used to make the meaning of a verb more specific is called an **adverb**. The word **adverb** means near a verb. Adverbs usually modify by showing how, when, where, or to what degree. Many adverbs are formed by adding *-ly* to the end of the word.

- Adverbs that show *how* or *in what manner* are called **adverbs of manner.**
    - swiftly, easily, carefully, slowly, promptly, thus

He walked **rapidly.** They are waiting **quietly.**
He walked **slowly.** They are waiting **together.**
He walked **constantly.** They are waiting **anxiously**.

- Those that show *when* are called **adverbs of time.**
    - yesterday, now, daily, soon, tomorrow, today, never,
    - immediately, often, hereafter, presently

He walked **yesterday.** They are waiting **presently.**
He walked **today.** They are waiting **now.**

- Those that show *where* are called **adverbs of place.**
    - here, everywhere, nowhere, there, backward,
    - forward, ashore, away

He walked **backward.** They are waiting **there.**
He walked **away.** They are waiting **here.**

- An **adverb of degree** answers the questions *How much?* or *To what extent?*
    - very, exceedingly, uncommonly

He was **very** tired. They are **exceedingly** thankful.
He was **too** tired. They are **uncommonly** joyful.

EXERCISE 48: IDENTIFYING ADVERBS: Underline the adverbs in the following sentences. On the line, write the verb each adverb modifies.

Ex.: The horses galloped wildly away. ______galloped______

______galloped______

1. Apples were scattered everywhere. ____________________
2. The officers handled the men roughly. ____________________
3. Mr. Smith formerly lived there. ____________________

____

4. The sun rose pleasantly on the village. ____________________
5. The horse suddenly ran away. ____________________

____

6. You all did love him once. ____________________
7. A light, swift boat sped northward. ____________________

EXERCISE 49: 1) If the word is an adjective, change it into an adverb. If the word is an adverb, change it into an adjective. 2) For each adjective and adverb, write a sentence. The first has been done for you. (Create your own sentences for number one.)

1. lazy (The *lazy* dog slept all day.) lazily (The dog *lazily* shifted his position.)

____

____

____

2. remarkable ____________________

____

____

____

3. angry ____________________

____

____

____

PREPOSITIONS

Prepositions are words that show the relation between different words of a sentence.

Prepositions are used to begin a prepositional phrase. Prepositions are usually placed *before* the word they join to the rest of the sentence. The word which prepositions join to the rest of the sentence is called the **object of the preposition.** It is a noun or pronoun. In between the preposition and the object of the preposition there may be articles or adjectives.

A prepositional phrase is considered extra information in the sentence.

> We need men **(*of* courage).**
> These children write **(*with* care).**
> The athlete was eager **(*for* the challenge).**

- The word *of* shows the relation between the noun *courage* and the noun *men*. The words *of courage* show **what kind** of men we need.
- The word *with* shows the relation between the noun *care* and the verb *write*. The words *with care* show **how** the children write.
- The word *for* shows the relation between the noun *challenge* and the adjective *eager*. The words *for the challenge* show in **what respect** the athlete is eager.

Sometimes the preposition comes after its object, especially in questions.

> **What are you talking about?**

These words are all used as **prepositions**:

about	among	beside	for	over	until
above	around	besides	from	through	unto
across	at	between	in	throughout	up
after	before	beyond	into	till	upon
against	behind	by	of	to	with
along	below	down	off	toward	within
amid	beneath	except	on	under	without

EXERCISE 50: Underline the preposition in each sentence. Place a set of parentheses around the prepositional phrases in each sentence.

1. The large sailboat in the harbor was anchored by the opening of the bay.
2. After dinner we can roast marshmallows over the fire.
3. My brother likes skateboarding at the skate park with his friends.
4. On my way I will stop at the store for groceries.
5. In the store window, you can see all the items for sale.

about	among	beside	for	over	until
above	around	besides	from	through	unto
across	at	between	in	throughout	up
after	before	beyond	into	till	upon
against	behind	by	of	to	with
along	below	down	off	toward	within
amid	beneath	except	on	under	without

EXERCISE 51: Fill in the blanks with suitable prepositions.

1. When Benjamin Franklin was seventeen, he ran away _________ his home _________ Boston.
2. He first went _________ New York _________ a sailing vessel.
3. Not finding work, he started _________ foot _________ Philadelphia.
4. When he got there, his clothes were spattered _________ mud, and _________ each arm, he carried a long roll _________ bread that he had just bought.
5. A girl named Deborah Read laughed _________ him as he trudged _________ the street, but a few years _________ this, she became his wife.

PREPOSITIONS OR ADVERBS

Some of the words listed as prepositions are often used as adverbs. It is use that determines what part of speech a word is in a given sentence.

Prepositions always have objects.

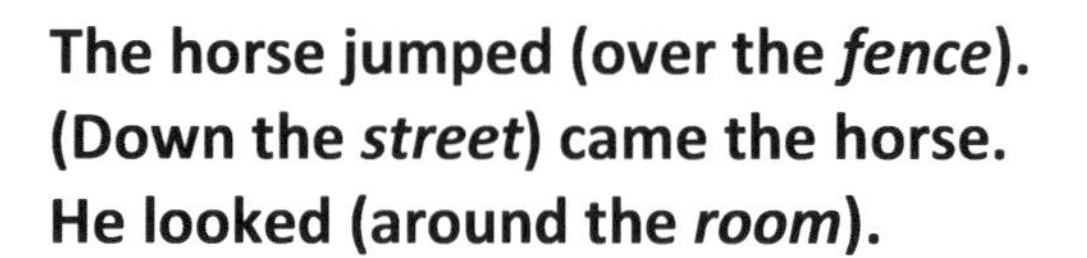

The horse jumped (over the *fence*). — *Fence* is the object of the preposition *over*.
(Down the *street*) came the horse. — *Street* is the object of the preposition *down*.
He looked (around the *room*). — *Room* is the object of the preposition *around*.

Adverbs modify verbs and tell how, where, when, why, under what condition, and to what degree.

The horse jumped *up*. — *Up* is an adverb.
***Down* came the horse.** — *Down* is an adverb.
He looked *around*. — *Around* is an adverb.

Sometimes a word that looks like a preposition is followed by a noun and yet is really an adverb.

The child knocked *over* a chair. — *Over* is an adverb.
The child did go over the chair.

If this sentence is written, *"The child knocked a chair over,"* we see that *chair* is the object of the verb and that *over* is an adverb. Note: Adverbs can be moved around in a sentence.

EXERCISE 52: On the line, write whether the italicized words are adverbs or prepositions.

1. For further particulars, inquire *within*. ____________________
2. Mr. Hatch will return *within* an hour. ____________________
3. The boy ran *up* the hill. ____________________
4. Run *up* the flag. ____________________
5. The carpenter fell *off* the house. ____________________
6. Suddenly, one of the wheels came *off*. ____________________
7. We shall come back *before* dinner. ____________________
8. I have seen that man *before*. ____________________
9. He turned on the alarm. ____________________
10. The dog stood *on* the grass. ____________________

WRITING WITH MODIFIERS

Read the following sentences. Which sentences appeal strongly to your feelings?

- **A woman fell.**
- **A frail, little, old woman, dressed in shabby clothes, fell at the street corner.**
- **A tall, stout woman, loaded with bundles of every size and shape, fell as she was stepping from a car.**
- **A dainty, graceful young woman fell into the water as she was stepping from a canoe.**

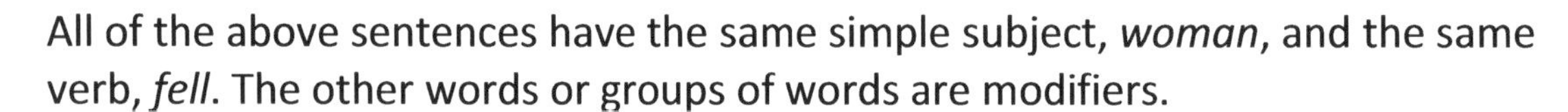

All of the above sentences have the same simple subject, *woman*, and the same verb, *fell*. The other words or groups of words are modifiers.

➢ **SENTENCE WRITING PRACTICE 13**: For each of the following simple sentences, compose a sentence that is more interesting and more vivid by adding adjectives, adverbs, prepositional phrases, and dependent clauses. Try to add at least two modifiers to each subject and two to each verb. See the example sentences above.

1. The bell rang.

2. The wind whispered.

3. Spiders floated.

CONJUNCTIONS

Study the italicized words in these sentences.

Was the horse injured in the barn *or* on the road?
The pig *and* the goat are outside of the barn.
The other animals are outside *because* they are enjoying the daylight.

In the first sentence, *in the barn* and *on the road* are connected by *or*. In the second sentence, *the pig* and *the goat* are connected by *and*. In the third, *The other animals are outside* and *they are enjoying the daylight* are connected by *because*.

And, or, and *because* are all **conjunctions**. They join words and groups of words in a sentence.

There are different kinds of conjunctions. The most common are the coordinating conjunctions, easily remembered by FANBOYS:

for, and, nor, but, or, yet, so

Coordinating conjunctions join words, phrases, or clauses that are equal.

We may also use **subordinating conjunctions** to join groups of words in sentences. Subordinating conjunctions come at the beginning of dependent clauses and join dependent clauses to independent clauses. Clauses that contain subordinating conjunctions cannot stand alone; the subordinating conjunction makes the clause dependent, by definition.

The other animals are outside.	Independent clause	Can stand alone
Because they are enjoying the daylight	Dependent clause	Cannot stand alone

Below is a list of subordinating conjunctions.

after	once	until
although	provided that	when
as	rather than	whenever
because	since	where
before	so that	whereas
even if	than	wherever
even though	that	whether
if	though	while
in order that	unless	why

EXERCISE 53: Underline the conjunctions in these sentences.

1. Georgia and Alabama produce much cotton.
2. George Washington was skillful but cautious.
3. We stayed because the weather was stormy.
4. La Salle was a bold and tireless explorer.
5. He sailed up the lake and down the river.
6. He kept on though it was cold and stormy.
7. Men never succeed unless they try.
8. I will talk with you, but I will not eat with you.
9. The earth was bright, and the sky was blue.
10. Do you intend to be a lawyer or a doctor?

EXERCISE 54: Fill in the blanks with coordinating conjunctions.

1. Will school open on Monday ____________ Tuesday?
2. Fred went fishing, _____________ he caught nothing.
3. Christmas came, _____________ school was closed.
4. The hammer has been lost ____________ stolen.
5. It rained very hard, ____________ I had an umbrella.
6. Shall I boil ____________ bake the potatoes?
7. Clara finished her work ___________ went out to play.
8. Who found the bracelet, Anna ____________ Emily?
9. Are the apples in the house ___________ in the barn?
10. He will arrive soon ___________ the plane isn't late.

INTERJECTIONS

In the following sentences, which words are used independently?

Hooray! I got the promotion!
Oh, this is a terrible accident!
Alas, the poor animal is dead!
Hello! Is this Mr. Smith?

Notice that the words *hooray*, *oh*, *alas*, and *hello* are used independently to express joy, surprise, sorrow, or impatience. They are called interjections. **Interjection** means thrown in.

An **interjection** is an exclamatory word used to express sudden or strong feeling.

EXERCISE 55: Underline the interjections in the sentences below. On the line, write what feeling you think each interjection expresses.

1. Pshaw! That's no reason. ______________________
2. Alas! What will become of me now? ______________________
3. Oh my goodness, what will she say to this? ______________________
4. Hooray! I've caught a fish! ______________________
5. Oh! I'm thankful he is gone! ______________________
6. Aye, tear down her horrible sign! ______________________
7. Oh that the waves were flowing over me! ______________________
8. O Father! I hear the sound of fireworks. ______________________
9. Goodbye! Come again soon! ______________________
10. Help! Somebody help me! ______________________

PATTERN ONE: SIMPLE SENTENCES

Now that we understand what the subject of a sentence is, what an intransitive verb or verb phrase is, and what a modifier is, we will look at the first of the five basic sentence patterns in English.

Pattern One: (Subject + Verb): The simplest pattern is pattern one, which consists of a subject and a predicate made of an intransitive verb that does not require a complement.

> **The kindergarten children were playing noisily.**
> **We have been playing since dinnertime.**
> **I was playing outside in the rain.**

Once the modifiers are removed from the sentences above, including prepositional phrases, we see that all of the sentences above follow pattern one—subject + intransitive verb.

Children	were playing
We	have been playing
I	was playing

EXERCISE 56: Place a vertical line | between the subject and predicate. Place parentheses around the prepositional phrases.

1. Fleming awoke at six o'clock.
2. Her eyes twinkle like a star.
3. The bread browned in the oven.
4. Our dance class practiced for our instructor.
5. The baseball team played until the sun went down.

- **SENTENCE WRITING PRACTICE 14:** Use the verbs given to compose sentences with a simple subject and a simple verb. Feel free to change the verb tense.

1. froze

____

____

2. rode

____

____

PATTERN TWO: DIRECT OBJECTS

Pattern Two: (Subject + Transitive Verb + Direct Object)
The second sentence pattern consists of a subject, a transitive verb, and a direct object.

We break the ice.	We break what?	The answer is the **ice**.
He moves the table.	He moves what?	The answer is the **table**.
He slammed the door.	He slammed what?	The answer is the **door**.

In each of the sentences, the verb is **transitive** and the answer is the direct object. A **direct object** (DO) is a noun, pronoun, or group of words acting as a noun that receives the action of a verb.

EXERCISE 57: Place a vertical line (|) between the subject and verb. Underline the direct object. If the subject is an understood *you*, place the line before the verb.

1. James Fennimore Cooper wrote adventure stories.
2. The poet Whittier once taught school.
3. Do not trouble him.
4. They want him and me.
5. Study the material for your test tomorrow.

EXERCISE 58: On the line, write if the sentence is Pattern One or Pattern Two.

1. Pizarro, a Spanish adventurer, conquered Peru. ____________________
2. The traveler departed without delay. ____________________
3. The lilacs bloomed in the backyard. ____________________
4. Put away your books. ____________________
5. In the Sahara, the date trees blossom in April. ____________________

➢ **SENTENCE WRITING PRACTICE 15:** Write two sentences, each with a direct object.

1. saw

____

____

2. cooked

____

____

PATTERN THREE: PREDICATE ADJECTIVES

Pattern Three: (Subject + Intransitive Verb + Predicate Adjective)

We have found that many **intransitive** verbs make complete sense by themselves without the help of any other word or words.

Trees grow. **Winds blow.** **The rope broke**.

On the other hand a **transitive** verb cannot make a complete assertion unless the receiver of the action is named. The thought is not complete without some word to name the person or thing that receives the action. Any word that is necessary to complete or fill out the meaning of a verb is called a **complement**, meaning that which completes. In the case of a transitive verb, the complement is called the direct object.

A few intransitive verbs (primarily the linking verbs) also do not make sense unless followed by a complement. If we hear the words *He is*, we ask *is what*?

He is rich.
They became sailors.
You look happy.
He seems sad.

The verbs *is, look, became***,** and *seems* do not make a complete predicate by themselves. The words *rich, sailors*, *happy,* and *sad* are **complements** because they complete the assertion.

The complement of an intransitive verb is often called a **subject complement** and renames or describes the subject.

The most important of these verbs is *be* (am, are, is, was, were, be, being, been). *Be* is also known as a linking verb because its only job is to link the subject and predicate. Other common **linking verbs** are *appear, become, feel, grow, look, remain, seem, smell, sound,* and *taste.*

The complement of an intransitive verb is sometimes an adjective.

The children were *happy*. **The boy seems *homesick*.**
His hands are *clean*. **That man looks *cheerful*.**
The water pail is *full*. **He became very *strong*.**

In each sentence above, an adjective is completing the predicate. An adjective that completes the predicate and explains the subject is called a **predicate adjective**. Predicate adjective and subject complement are two terms for the same thing.

EXERCISE 59: Place a vertical line between the subject and the verb. Underline the adjective that completes the predicate in each of these sentences.

1. Some men | are <u>generous.</u>
2. The weather is cold!
3. Do not look so cross.
4. The room seems damp.
5. His gallant horse was dead.
6. I am terribly anxious.
7. November woods are bare.
8. He became too careless.
9. He appears very much discouraged.
10. The air has grown very misty.

EXERCISE 60: Construct five sentences that have adjectives as complements. Choose from among the adjectives below.

pleasant	sad	blue	heavy	round	busy
polite	brittle	small	lazy	smooth	shaggy

1. ______________________________

____

2. ______________________________

____

3. ______________________________

____

4. ______________________________

____

5. ______________________________

____

PATTERN THREE: PREDICATE NOMINATIVES

Pattern Three: (Subject + Intransitive Verb + Predicate Nominative)

The complement of a linking verb can also be a noun.

> **Lions are immense *cats*.**
> **She became *president*.**

A noun that completes the predicate and renames the subject is called a **predicate noun** or a **predicate nominative**.

EXERCISE 61: Fill in each blank with a suitable complement, and tell whether you used a predicate noun or predicate adjective.

1. The fields are ____________________. ____________________
2. The weather is ____________________. ____________________
3. A noun is ____________________. ____________________
4. My hands are ____________________. ____________________
5. Chicago is a large ____________________. ____________________
6. This story is very ____________________. ____________________
7. Harvey is very ____________________. ____________________
8. The sky looks ____________________. ____________________
9. Mining is a dangerous ____________________. ____________________
10. The robin is a cheerful ____________________. ____________________

EXERCISE 62: Construct two sentences, each having one of the nouns below as a complement.

president king season neighbor

1. ____

____

2. ____

____

PATTERN FOUR: INDIRECT OBJECT

Pattern Four: (Subject +Transitive Verb + Indirect Object + Direct Object)

Pattern Four sentences contain an extra noun or pronoun in the predicate after a transitive verb. This noun or pronoun is called the **indirect object**.

Albert lent his computer.
Albert lent me his computer.

In the first sentence, the transitive verb *lent* takes the direct object *computer*. The computer is the thing that is lent. In the second sentence, the pronoun *me* is added to the verb *lent* to show the person to whom Albert lent his computer. A noun or a pronoun that receives the direct object is called an **indirect object**. If you can place this noun within a prepositional phrase by rearranging the words in the sentence, it is an indirect object.

The following verbs may take an indirect object:

allow, assign, bring, buy, deny, do, fetch, forgive, furnish, give, get, hand, leave, lend, make, offer, owe, pay, promise, refuse, render, sell, send, show, spare, teach, tell, write

EXERCISE 63: Underline the direct objects, and circle the indirect objects.

1. I paid the cashier fifty dollars.
2. Who taught you grammar?
3. The usher handed each visitor a program.
4. Thrice they offered him a kingly crown.
5. I built my grandmother a beautiful house.
6. Franklin rendered the colonies a great service.
7. O, give me my lowly thatched cottage again.
8. His mother gave him pocket money.
9. Constant success only shows us one side of life.
10. Do not lend him money.

PATTERN FIVE: OBJECT COMPLEMENTS

Pattern Five: (Subject + Transitive Verb + Direct Object + Object Complement)

Like the Pattern Four sentence, the Pattern Five sentence is made of a subject and verb followed by two nouns. One noun is the direct object, and the other is the object complement. The **object complement** refers to the direct object and tells what it has become.

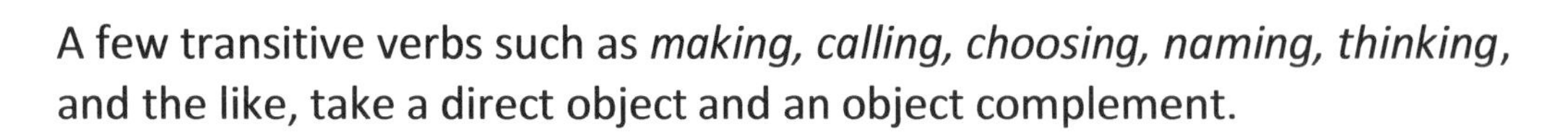

A few transitive verbs such as *making, calling, choosing, naming, thinking*, and the like, take a direct object and an object complement.

1. The club elected Stephanie *president*.	President is the object complement.
2. They have made Jenkins *foreman*.	Foreman is the object complement.
3. I consider the man *trustworthy*.	Trustworthy is the object complement.

If we omit the words *president, foreman*, and *trustworthy*, the above sentences do not make sense. These words complete the meaning of the above verbs and are, therefore, a complement. In sentences 1 and 2, the object complements are nouns. In sentence 3, the object complement is an adjective.

These words also explain the direct objects *Stephanie, Jenkins*, and *man*. For this reason, the words *president, foreman*, and *trustworthy* are called object complements. The object complement is necessary for the object to be complete, for without the object complement, the object doesn't make sense. Consider the following ungrammatical sentences. In each, the question *what?* remains.

1. *The club elected Stephanie.	**The club elected Stephanie what?**
2. *They have made Jenkins.	**They have made Jenkins what?**
3. *I consider the man.	**I consider the man what?**

EXERCISE 64: Underline the object complements in the following sentences. On the line write whether the complement is a noun or adjective. (Complete on the following page.)

1. The umpire decided the game lost. ______________________________
2. Everybody thought him insane. ______________________________
3. He painted his house white. ______________________________
4. Do you consider your friend a poet? ______________________________
5. He makes me angry. ______________________________
6. I count my health my greatest wealth. ______________________________
7. They named their daughter Tuesdae. ______________________________

EXERCISE 65: Label the sentence Pattern One, Pattern Two, or Pattern Three.

Pattern One: (Subject + Verb)
Pattern Two: (Subject + Transitive Verb + Direct Object)
Pattern Three: (Subject + Intransitive Verb + Predicate Adjective)
Pattern Three: (Subject + Intransitive Verb + Predicate Nominative)

1. The horse is black. ____________________
2. My head aches. ____________________
3. Do not touch me. ____________________
4. The fishermen caught nothing. ____________________
5. Tadpoles become frogs. ____________________
6. They disappeared. ____________________
7. The bird died. ____________________
8. Glass feels smooth. ____________________
9. You seem weary. ____________________
10. Do not trouble him. ____________________

➢ **SENTENCE WRITING PRACTICE 16:** Write two sentences, using the verbs given. Compose each with both a direct object and object complement.

1. named

____

____

____

2. called

____

____

____

CLAUSES AND PHRASES

A **phrase** is a group of words functioning as one unit.

giraffe	the tall skinny giraffe
car	the blue race car

A **clause** is a group of words that contains a subject and verb. Some clauses are independent; some are dependent. An independent clause is one that expresses a complete thought and can stand alone. A dependent (or subordinate clause) must be joined to an independent clause because it does not express a complete thought.

We need motivated employees.

Motivated employees is a phrase.

We need employees who are motivated.

Who are motivated is a dependent clause.

The group of words *who are motivated* is not a phrase because it has a subject and a predicate or verb phrase. Here, the subject is the pronoun *who* and the verb phrase is *are motivated.* Such a group of words is called **a clause.**

A boy who is studious usually succeeds. — **Who is studious** is a clause. (subject and verb)

A studious boy usually succeeds. — **A studious boy** is a phrase. (noun only; lacks a verb)

EXERCISE 66: Tell whether the italicized group of words is a phrase or clause.

1. The lady *in the black dress* was Mrs. Robinson. ________________
2. The lady *who wore the black dress* was Mrs. Robinson. ________________
3. Please return the book *that you borrowed*. ________________
4. A dog *that is always barking* does not often bite. ________________
5. The evil *that men do* lives after them. ________________
6. The man *who married Pocahontas* was John Rolfe. ________________
7. People *who are lazy* often take the most pains. ________________
8. We took the road *that led directly* to New Haven. ________________
9. *When the gate opened*, the procession filed in. ________________
10. Where is the house *whose chimney was blown down*? ________________

ADJECTIVE CLAUSES

A clause that modifies a noun or pronoun is called an **adjective clause**. An adjective clause is a clause that is used like an adjective.

A king *who always complains* is never respected.
I remember the house *where the princess was born*.
Uneasy lies the head *that wears a crown*.

An **adjective clause** is usually introduced by a relative pronoun, such as who (whose, whom), which, or that, or by a relative adverb, such as where, when, or why. It usually follows the noun it modifies.

EXERCISE 67: Underline the adjective clauses. On the line, write the noun or pronoun each modifies.

1. The man who hesitates is lost. ____________________
2. This is the house that Jack built. ____________________
3. Am I the person to whom you refer? ____________________
4. I know the place where the strawberries grow. ____________________
5. The tiger is a beast that kills without pity. ____________________
6. Nobody wants a farm that produces no crops. ____________________
7. Is that the man whose house was burned? ____________________
8. Evils that cannot be cured must be endured. ____________________
9. The only jewel which will not decay is knowledge. ____________________
10. I remember the lilacs where the robins nested. ____________________

EXERCISE 68: Fill in the following blanks with adjective clauses.

1. People ____ need a physician.
2. You have not returned the book ____.
3. I have lost all the money ____.
4. Have you tried the sled ____?
5. We took the road ____.
6. Students ____ will not graduate.

ADVERBIAL CLAUSES

An **adverbial clause** is a dependent clause that functions like an adverb. An **adverbial clause** is usually introduced by a subordinating conjunction, such as *although, because, if, lest, than, that, until, ere, while, before, after*, or *as*, or by an adverb, such as *where, wherever, when,* or *whenever.*
An adverbial clause can modify a verb, an adjective, or an adverb.
Remember, a dependent clause has a subject and a verb, but does not stand alone as a sentence.

The toy soldier died *where he fell.* *Where he fell* is an adverbial clause.

In the following sentences, the same thought is expressed in two ways:

1. Weeds grow fast in wet weather.
2. Weeds grow fast when the weather is wet.

In the first sentence, the verb *grow* is modified by the adverbial prepositional phrase *in wet weather*; in the second, the same meaning is expressed by the clause *when the weather is wet*. Both tell when weeds grow fast; both function as adverbs. The first sentence has an adverb phrase (in wet weather), and the second an adverbial clause (when the weather is wet).

Study these sentences until you clearly see that the adverbial clause really modifies the verb in the main clause:

1. Come *when I call you*. (Come when?)

2. Put the book *where you found it*. (Put it where?)

3. Keep your seat *until the car stops*. (Keep it how long?)

4. You must do *as I do*. (Must do how?)

5. My cousin arrived *as I was leaving*. (Arrived when?)

6. *Because it was very late*, I came away. (Came away why?)

7. Mr. Jones resigned *because his health was poor*. (Resigned for what reason?)

8. George is going to Europe *that he may continue his studies*. (Is going for what purpose?)

9. I will come *if I am invited*. (Will come on what condition?)

EXERCISE 69: In the following sentences, change the italicized phrases to adverbial clauses.

1. We took a drive *after dinner*.

____

____

2. Few men are idle *in good times*.

____

____

3. *Upon my return*, I will read you the letter.

____

____

4. Do your errands *before school*.

____

____

5. Some boys talked *during Mr. Brown's lecture*.

____

____

EXERCISE 70: Underline the adverbial clauses in the following sentences.

1. Strike while the iron is hot.
2. Make hay while the sun shines.
3. Be silent that you may hear.
4. Fools rush in where angels fear to tread.
5. Caesar had a fever when he was in Spain.
6. Smooth runs the water where the brook is deep.
7. William Cullen Bryant wrote poetry when he was a boy.
8. The raft went very well until it met a swift current.
9. Childhood shows the man as morning shows the day.
10. If a man empties his purse into his head, no one can take it away from him.

NOUN CLAUSES

These two sentences express the same meaning in different ways:

1. William's success is very obvious.
2. That William is successful is very obvious.

In sentence 1, the noun phrase *William's success* is the subject. In 2, the clause *that William is successful* takes the place of *William's success* as the subject. It is plain to see that the clause is used like a noun since it is the subject of the sentence. Such clauses are called **noun clauses**.

- A **noun clause** is a whole clause that is used like a noun.

  ***That I was mistaken* is evident.**

- A noun clause is often used as the subject or the object of a verb.

  ***That he failed* was unfortunate. (Subject)**
  We know *where you are going*. (Object)

- The conjunction *that* is often omitted before a noun clause.

  I know (that) ***he will be there*.**

- A noun clause is sometimes the object of a preposition.

  They came *to where the young child lay*.

EXERCISE 71: Underline the noun clause. On the line, write subject or object depending on the way the noun clause is used in the sentence.

1. He thinks that I am mistaken. ______________________________
2. That he speaks the truth is certain. ______________________________
3. Every man ate what he wanted. ______________________________
4. How you do it is a mystery to me. ______________________________
5. That Mrs. Hanson won is now acknowledged. ______________________________

EXERCISE 72: Expand the italicized words into noun clauses.

1. I predict *a change in the weather.*

____

2. He promised *an early reply.*

____

3. Everything indicates *a cold winter.*

____

4. The jury believed *the man guilty.*

____

5. We expect *an improvement in business.*

____

EXERCISE 73: Underline the noun clause in the sentence, and on the line, write the part of speech it acts as.

1. He knew that the car was broken. ____________________
2. His promise was that he would return soon. ____________________
3. The jury believed that the woman was guilty. ____________________
4. My expectation is that my brother will arrive today. ____________________
5. That the earth is round can be easily shown. ____________________
6. The probability is that it will rain tomorrow. ____________________
7. Many believe that the soul is immortal. ____________________
8. I dream that everyone might live free. ____________________

PREPOSITIONAL PHRASES

A **phrase** is a group of related words having neither subject nor predicate and is equivalent to a single part of speech. A phrase that consists of a preposition and its object (with modifiers) is called a **prepositional phrase**. Prepositional phrases begin with the preposition, and often end with a noun.

- A prepositional phrase can act as an **adjective**.

She is a wealthy person.	wealthy = adjective modifying *person*
She is a person of wealth.	of wealth = prepositional phrase modifying p*erson*

- A prepositional phrase can act as an **adverb**.

The boy writes carefully.	carefully = adverb modifying *writes*
The boy writes with care.	with care = prepositional phrase modifying writes

Common Prepositions

about	above	across	after	against	around	at
before	behind	below	between	by	from	for
in	inside	into	of	off	on	out
over	through	until	up	with	within	without

EXERCISE 74: Place parentheses around the prepositional phrases. On the line, write whether each phrase is used as an adjective or an adverb.

1. Little Jack Horner sat in a corner. ______________________________
2. Jack and Jill went up the hill. ______________________________
3. My brother will return in two weeks. ______________________________
4. The dial on this radio is broken. ______________________________
5. The chairs on the veranda are new. ______________________________
6. That woman works with great energy. ______________________________

EXERCISE 75: In the following sentences, replace the adjective or adverb with a prepositional phrase.

Ex.: Moscow is a Russian city. Moscow is a city **in Russia**.

1. Who is that dark-eyed girl?

____

2. Jackson was a courageous man.

____

3. Some pets learn easily.

____

VERBALS

Verbals are forms of verbs that act like other parts of speech in sentences. They can stand alone in a sentence or begin phrases; however, they are not the main verb or the simple predicate of the sentence.

There are three kinds of verbals: **participles**, **gerunds**, and **infinitives**.

A **participle** is a verb that can be used as an adjective. Participles can end in *-ing, -en, -n, -ed, -d,* or *-t.*

A *flying* squirrel zipped from tree to tree.

The participle is the third form of the verb, or the past participle.

A **gerund** is a verb form ending in *-ing* that can be used as a noun. It can be used as the subject, direct object, or predicate noun of the sentence.

***Walking* is considered excellent exercise.** (subject)
Stephanie likes *walking*. (direct object)

An **infinitive** is a verb form that often begins with *to* and can be used as a noun, adjective, or adverb.

***To dance* with you would be wonderful.** (noun, subject)
I like *to dance*. (noun, direct object)

EXERCISE 76: Underline the verbal in the sentence. On the line, write participle, gerund, or infinitive.

1. My sister wants to shop after school. ______________________
2. Shopping is her favorite hobby. ______________________
3. The melting candle dripped on the tablecloth. ______________________
4. I have no one to decorate the gym with me. ______________________
5. The exhausted children napped on the floor. ______________________

VERBAL PHRASES

Verbals can be used to begin phrases in sentences. These **verbal phrases** then act like nouns, adjectives, or adverbs depending on how they are used.

Participial phrases begin with participles and are used like adjectives, modifying nouns in the sentence.

The girl *walking the dog* looks like my cousin.

Gerund phrases begin with gerunds and are used like nouns in the sentence.

***Walking to school* is great exercise.**

Infinitive phrases begin with infinitives and are used as nouns or modifiers (adjectives and adverbs).

It is important *to work diligently*.
My parents wanted *to give me a present.*

EXERCISE 77: Underline the verbal phrase. On the line, write whether the phrase is a participial, gerund, or infinitive phrase.

1. Helping prepare dinner will make your family happy. ______________________

2. Setting the table is a great start. ______________________

3. My family likes to cook together. ______________________

4. We watch my dad grilling in the backyard. ______________________

5. To make a salad, my mom gathers vegetables from our garden.

____

MORE ON PARTICIPLES

There are two simple participles, the present participle and the past participle, and a third type that is known as the perfect participle.

Present Participles express an incomplete or continuing action: ***driving, helping.***

Past Participles express completed action: ***driven, helped.***

Perfect Participles represent actions completed at some past time.

Having rested, we continued our journey.

EXERCISE 78: Underline the participle in the following sentences. On the line provided, tell whether it is a past participle, a present participle, or a perfect participle.

1. I saw her singing at her work. ____present____
2. Hannah is at the window binding shoes. ________________
3. Truth crushed to earth shall rise again. ________________
4. Circling above us, the black rooks fly. ________________
5. It is dangerous to live in a house built of glass. ________________
6. The deer saw the boat headed for her. ________________
7. 'Tis the last rose of summer, left blooming alone. ________________
8. Having seen the giant, the man was afraid. ________________
9. Often I sat in my room reading the greater part of the night.

   ____

10. The children coming home from school look in at the open door.

    ____

MORE ON GERUNDS

Many sentences may be composed with either a gerund or an infinitive.

Asking questions is easier than answering them. **(Gerunds.)**
To ask questions is easier than to answer them. **(Infinitives.)**

EXERCISE 79: In the following sentences, change the gerunds to infinitives, and the infinitives to gerunds.

1. Giving is better than receiving.

____

____

2. Walking several miles a day would do you good.

____

____

3. Knowing some trade is a great convenience.

____

____

4. I shall continue to study arithmetic.

____

____

5. Do you like writing essays?

____

____

MORE ON INFINITIVES

A verb that is used with a subject must agree with that subject in person and number. We say: *I run, he runs, he is,* and *they are*. This is not true for an infinitive no matter what the subject of the sentence may be; therefore, this verb form is called infinitive, the unlimited form.

I like **to run**.
He likes **to run**.
She likes **to run**.
We like **to run.**
They like **to run**

EXERCISE 80: Underline the infinitive phrase in each of the following sentences. On the line provided, tell whether each infinitive phrase is a subject or an object. The first one has been done for you.

1. They love <u>to see the flaming forge</u>. ______object______
2. To copy a whole page is rather tiresome. ____________________
3. To waste valuable time is unwise. ____________________
4. The carpenter decided to do the work alone. ____________________
5. I now tried to sit up and paddle the boat. ____________________
6. To escape from poverty is no easy matter. ____________________
7. I want to fly the plane by myself. ____________________
8. I attempted to land upon the Cape of the Woods. ____________________

PUNCTUATION

Punctuation marks help us know when to stop, start, and pause when we read sentences. They can indicate the beginnings and endings of clauses or phrases. They can also separate groups of words within a sentence to create a specific effect.

END MARKS

Review the following rules for end marks, and complete the exercise below.

End marks are used at the end of a complete sentence.

A declarative sentence ends with a period.	**(.)**
An abbreviation is followed by a period.	**(.)**
An interrogative sentence ends with a question mark.	**(?)**
An exclamatory sentence ends with an exclamation point.	**(!)**
An imperative sentence ends with a period or an exclamation point depending on the force used.	**(.)** or **(!)**

EXERCISE 81: Add the correct punctuation to the following sentences.

1. Hooray I found my laptop
2. My hand trembles
3. Is your name Jacob
4. Get away from the ledge
5. Sugar tastes sweet
6. Oh no the tire is flat
7. Will you have some
8. Turn off your phones
9. Are you finished with the job
10. Help me

COMMAS

Commas are used to separate words and groups of words in a sentence.

- Use commas to separate items in a series.

  She likes red, blue, and purple.

- Use commas to separate two or more adjectives of equal importance before a noun.

  He was an active, intelligent pet.

- Use a comma (and a coordinating conjunction) between independent clauses in a compound sentence.

  She likes her noodles with butter, but he likes his with sauce and cheese.

- Use commas to separate a non-essential clause from the rest of the sentence. (A non-essential clause can be removed from the sentence, and the sentence will still make sense.) **Fred, who lost his wallet, is doing extra chores for money.**

- Use a comma after introductory elements, including phrases of more than four words, or clauses.

  After the storm we played in the puddles. (No comma needed, < 5 words)

  Before the start of the school year, you need to review your grammar.

  Because it is a holiday, we are not working today.

- Use a comma to set apart a word or phrase used when directly addressing someone.

  Excuse me, sir; can you point me to the train station?
  Daughter, you have made me proud.

EXERCISE 82: Add commas to the following sentences.

1. I admire a person who can speak two languages play an instrument and cook a gourmet meal.
2. Before you go to school get dressed eat breakfast and brush your teeth.
3. The marching band played during halftime and the cheerleaders performed too.
4. After the war ended Washington retired to Mt. Vernon.
5. Dad may I go to the mall?
6. Take your own time Annie.
7. Come into the garden Maud.
8. Do your very best my child each day of your life.

SEMI-COLONS

Semi-colons are used to separate groups of words and clauses in a sentence.

- Use a semi-colon to separate independent clauses.

She likes chocolate ice cream; he likes vanilla ice cream.

- Use a semi-colon plus a conjunctive adverb and a comma to separate independent clauses.

She likes chocolate ice cream; however, she doesn't like chocolate cake.
She likes chocolate ice cream; she doesn't, however, like chocolate cake.
(Note: Like other adverbs, the conjunctive adverb can move in the sentence.)

- Use semi-colons to separate items in a series if the items contain commas.

For my birthday, I want vanilla ice cream, my sister's favorite; chocolate milk, my brother's favorite; and strawberry cake, my favorite.

The cities under flood watch are Dallas, Texas; Houston, Texas; and Austin, Texas.

EXERCISE 83: Add semi-colons and commas to the following sentences.

1. Stephen likes salad Jennifer likes chocolate.
2. I put off completing my homework therefore I was unprepared for the quiz.
3. My brother plays the violin I play the piano.
4. I need to travel to Los Angeles California Dallas Texas and Miami Florida.
5. Ted wanted to play baseball however he had to take care of his dog.
6. Jonathan plays the piano he wants to play the clarinet.
7. The test was extremely difficult however I had studied for it.
8. I plan to run a marathon next month therefore I need to exercise more frequently.
9. The movie was amazing I fell asleep however before the ending.
10. Oscar the cat is adorable however he is very mischievous.

DIRECT QUOTATIONS

When the exact words of one person are repeated by another person, those words are said to be quoted, and such a group of words is called a **direct quotation**. Quoted words, when written, are enclosed by **quotation marks**.

Learn these rules for writing direct quotations:

- A direct quotation is enclosed by quotation marks.
  "Hurry home!" she screamed.

- In a sentence, it begins with a capital letter.
  He answered, "Thunderstorms are expected tomorrow."

- It is usually separated from the rest of the sentence by a comma or another punctuation mark.
  "When would you like to visit?" asked Mrs. Smith.
  "What a beautiful day," she sighed.

- When the quotation is divided, both parts are enclosed by quotation marks, and the words between the parts are usually enclosed by commas.
  "The twins," said Mother, "are fast asleep."

EXERCISE 84: Add quotation marks and other punctuation marks where they are needed.

1. No other tree is as wonderful as I am said the pine tree.
2. Be sure my child said the widow to her little daughter that you always do just as you are told.
3. Why did you not lay up food during the summer inquired the ant of the grasshopper.
4. But it is so delightful to swim about in the water said the duckling.
5. Once upon a time a little leaf was heard to sigh and cry as leaves often do when a gentle wind is about and the twig said what is the matter little leaf

   The leaf said the wind has just told me that one day it would pull me off and throw me down on the ground to wither
6. I am not a bird, but a mouse said the bat.
7. Emerson said Light is the best policeman.
8. I would rather be right than be President said Henry Clay.

INDIRECT QUOTATIONS

Notice whether each of these quotations gives the exact words or merely the thought of another.

1. Robert said, "I'm ready."
2. Robert said that he was ready.
3. Father asked me, "Where did you find it?"
4. Father asked me where I found it.

Sometimes, a quotation gives the exact words of another person as in sentences 1 and 3; sometimes, it gives the thought but not the exact words as in sentences 2 and 4.

A quotation that gives the thought, but not the exact words, is called an **indirect quotation**.

An indirect quotation:

- Is not enclosed by quotation marks.
- Does not begin with a capital letter.
- Is not separated from the rest of the sentence by a comma.
- Is not followed by a question mark, even when a question is implied.

EXERCISE 85: Write whether each quotation is direct or indirect; then add punctuation. The first has been done for you.

1. "Where do you live?" asked the stranger of Alice. ______direct______
2. Don't fail boys said Matthew to come over this evening ____________
3. We asked John where he was going so early ____________
4. Get ready cried Standish to his men ____________
5. The paper says that the weather will be colder tomorrow ____________
6. Tony exclaimed I am ready ____________
7. Robert exclaimed that he was ready too ____________
8. Margaret said I will come ____________
9. The other students said that they would come ____________
10. Mother asked me Did you clean your room ____________

CAPITALIZATION

The following begin with a capital letter:

- The first word of every sentence and the first word of every line of poetry.
  Come to the fair this weekend.

  I wandered lonely as a cloud
  That floats on high o'er vales and hills,

- The first word of every direct quotation.
  Her sister said, "Sarah, come here!"

- Proper nouns and proper adjectives. (Includes days and months, but not seasons.)
  Andrew Jackson **New York** **Thursday** **April** **summer**

- Titles of honor or office when used with a proper name.
  President Lincoln **General Wood** **secretary of state**

- Important words in the title of a book, composition, or organization. Note: Book titles are italicized.
  The Heart of Darkness ***The Escape of the Killer Noun*** **The Office of Marine Affairs**

- The words *North, South, East,* and *West* when denoting parts of the country, but not when denoting direction.
  They spent the winter in the South. **Cleveland is east of Chicago.**

- The pronoun I and the interjection O are always capitals.
  O, give me my lowly thatched cottage again. **It is I.**

- In a letter, the street address, the city and state, the country (if included), and the date.
  612 First Street
  Houston, TX USA
  January 1, 2022

  Greeting: Capitalize the first word and the name (or term) of the person you are addressing.
  Dear Sir, **Dear Madam,** **Dear Mrs. Jackson,** **To Whom It May Concern,**

  Closing: Capitalize the first word of the closing and your name.
  Your friend,
  Mike

EXERCISE 86: Below is a letter from Eugene Field to his sons. Circle all of the words that should be capitalized in the letter.

amsterdam, holland
november 8, 1899

dear boys,

i wonder whether you miss me as much as i miss you. i wish you were here in amsterdam with us, for it is a beautiful city, and it is full of curious sights. mrs. lynch has bought a pair of dutch wooden shoes to take to little leigh, and i have bought a funny old dutch watch.

tonight we go to london, and in the morning we shall be in the rooms where you were with us ten days ago. i shall expect to hear from each one of you once a week. meanwhile be courteous and attentive to professor and madame ruhle; when you play, play hard, when you study, study hard. you must take good care of your health, and be careful not to over exert yourself at the gymnasium. pinny must write to his aunt etta, melvin must write to mr. gray, and sometimes dady must write to his aunt carrie. on the other side of this letter are the office addresses. goodbye, my dear boys; i shall write again from london in a day or two.

affectionately,
eugene field

ANSWER KEY

EXERCISE 1

1. <u>President George Washington lived at Mt. Vernon</u>.
2. The tops of distant mountains.
3. <u>The daisy is yellow</u>.
4. Down the long, narrow street.
5. Rosebushes heavy with blossoms.
6. <u>The mist rose from the meadows</u>.
7. To hit the nail on the head.
8. <u>Modern ships cross the Atlantic in five days</u>.
9. My favorite novel.
10. <u>*To Kill a Mockingbird* is my favorite novel.</u>

EXERCISE 2

Answers will vary. Possible responses:

1. Chicago
2. Donald Trump
3. Christopher Columbus
4. A cruise ship

EXERCISE 3

Answers will vary. Possible responses.

1. is very large.
2. tastes delicious.
3. has a lot of cows.
4. is in the middle of a body of water.
5. flows quickly.
6. are very beautiful.

EXERCISE 4

Imitation sentences will vary. Some are suggested below.

1. Evangeline | cried.

Mary laughed.

2. Vast meadows | stretched over the horizon.

Large mountains peaked in the sky.

3. The chimney | filled with smoke.

The fireplace filled with flames.

4. The young woman | walked proudly through the village.

The small child ran quickly through the town.

EXERCISE 5

1. The little <u>boy</u> <u>rode</u> his scooter around the block.
2. Aunt <u>Susie</u> <u>bakes</u> the best cakes.
3. Several <u>children</u> from the neighborhood <u>were playing</u> near the fountain.
4. Many different <u>kinds</u> of monkeys <u>live</u> at the zoo.
5. <u>Video games</u> <u>can shorten</u> your attention span.

(*Video games* is a compound noun.)

EXERCISE 6

1. The beautiful princess | quickly climbed over the hill.
2. The astronaut | donned his spacesuit.
3. The children | slept quietly while the parents drove through the night.
4. The dog | jumped into the river to save his master.
5. My grandparents | successfully completed a twenty-six mile marathon last month.

EXERCISE 7

1. The farm boy goes over the hill.
2. The fire roared up the chimney.
3. A lofty mountain towered above their heads.
4. The soft and silent snow came down.
5. The ivy green is a rare old plant.

EXERCISE 8

Imitation sentences will vary. Some are suggested below.

1. Neil Armstrong was the first person to walk on the moon. Declarative

George Washington was the first US president.

2. What a great time we had last night!

Exclamatory

You are so lucky to win the lottery!

3. What causes the change of seasons?

Interrogative

Why is the sky blue?

4. Write your lesson on ruled paper.

Imperative

Ask me any questions.

5. I cut my finger!

Exclamatory

He wrecked his car!

6. O wind, that sings so loud a song!

Exclamatory

O rain, that lulls me into sweet slumber!

7. The dogs are barking again.

Declarative

The cats are fighting again.

8. Who has seen the wind?

Interrogative

Who has felt the rain?

9. Dare to do right! Dare to be true!

Imperative or exclamatory

Do the right thing!

10. You have a work that no other can do.

Declarative

Only you know what's in your heart.

EXERCISE 9

1. Did De Soto discover the Mississippi River?
2. Was the first school in Chicago opened in 1816?
3. Was Patrick Henry an eloquent speaker?
4. New Orleans is sometimes called the Crescent City.

EXERCISE 10

1. (You) | aim at perfection in everything.
2. (You) | do not look a gift horse in the mouth.
3. (You) | don't give up the ship.
4. Now, (you) | tell me all about the performance.
5. (You) | overcome evil with good.

EXERCISE 11

1. How small these apples are!
   Exclamatory
2. I can't believe it!
   Exclamatory
3. Insects visit flowers in search of honey.
   Declarative
4. Oases furnish resting places for travelers.
   Declarative
5. It was a cold, wet, rainy day.
   Declarative
6. Close the blinds, please.
   Imperative
7. Have you finished your geography homework?
   Interrogative

EXERCISE 12

1. England and Wales | have extensive copper mines.
   Compound subject
2. Susie | ate ice cream and enjoyed the summer night.
   Compound predicate
3. A fifteen-piece band | played and marched in the parade. Compound predicate
4. No tree or shrub | grew upon the surface of the island. Compound subject
5. More than four hundred people | gathered and piled into the auditorium. Compound predicate

EXERCISE 13

1. We went over the bridge, down the lane, and through the meadow.
2. The boys, the girls, and the parents enjoyed the camping trip.
3. The day was blustery, cold, and generally disagreeable.
4. The people shouted, waved their arms, and tried to express their joy.

EXERCISE 14

1. The night is dark, **and** I am far from home.
2. The shallows murmur, **but** the deeps are dumb.
3. The piper advanced; the children followed.
4. Hunger is the best sauce, **and** fatigue is the best pillow.
5. The students studied their lessons; **therefore**, they were ready for the quiz.

EXERCISE 15

1. He smiled when he saw me.
   complex
2. A fair face may hide a foul heart.
   simple
3. Hold the horse until I return.
   complex
4. Drowning men catch at straws.
   simple
5. The longest way around is the shortest way home.
   simple
6. He is a fine man although he is sad.
   complex
7. Inventors make many efforts before they succeed.
   complex
8. Unless you put on your coat, you will freeze.
   complex
9. While you were away, three marketers called.
   complex
10. The students failed because they did not study.
    complex

EXERCISE 16

Independent clause in bold. Dependent clause underlined.

1. **She has lived there** since she was born.
2. As the line tightened, **the trout leaped out of the water**.
3. As he approached the stream, **his heart began to thump**.
4. **She pushed up her sleeves** as though she were going to fight for the champion's belt.
5. **The swift phantom of the desert was gone** before we could get out heads out of the window.
6. **The goods** that were not sold **were packed away**.
7. After I had eaten my dinner, **I went out for a walk**.

EXERCISE 17

1. The house is beautiful. . — see
2. The sound of the music was terrible. — hear, hear
3. A gentle breeze was blowing. — touch
4. The fragrance of these flowers is delightful. — smell, see
5. The strength of the gorilla is very great. — think, see
6. The air resounded with the songs of the birds. — touch, hear, see
7. The clatter of the cars annoyed him. — hear, see
8. The sleigh bells were ringing. — hear
9. John, my brother, can learn his lessons in an hour. — see, see, think, think
10. Good health is better than wealth. — think, think

EXERCISE 18

1. Rockies	mountains
2. Alabama	state
3. November	month
4. Baltimore	city
5. Thursday	day

Proper nouns will vary. Examples include:
1. Main Street
2. Florida
3. The Bible
4. The Gulf of Mexico
5. Mount Everest

EXERCISE 19

1. churches	6. leaves
2. teeth	7. cities
3. stories	8. armies
4. pianos	9. monkeys
5. voices	10. thieves

EXERCISE 20

1. The whiteness of this paper is remarkable.
2. Washington's goodness was known by all.
3. Wisdom should always be pursued.
4. Pride goeth before destruction.
5. Beauty is its own reason for existence.
6. Education is the act of gaining knowledge.
7. Always speak the truth in love.
8. We should always practice moderation and relaxation.

EXERCISE 21

A	weariness	A	resistance
A	growth	C	sidewalk
C	child	C	carpet
A	childhood	C	boy
A	sickness	A	truth
C	book	C	telephone
A	anger	C	bacteria

EXERCISE 22

1. A herd of horses (**was**, were) seen on the desert.
2. The committee (**is**, are) meeting today.
3. The audience (**was**, were) very responsive to the performance.
4. Our football team (**is**, are) practicing hard to win.
5. The flock of geese (**was**, were) flying northward.
6. The orchestra (is, **are**) tuning their instruments.
7. A class of worried students (was, **were**) comparing notes before the test.

EXERCISE 23

1. singular
2. plural
3. singular
4. plural
5. singular

EXERCISE 24

1. singular
2. plural
3. singular or plural
4. singular
5. singular

EXERCISE 25

1. One boy, Charles White, was absent.
2. We went fishing yesterday, Frank and I.
3. Elias Howe, the inventor of the sewing machine, was once a poor man.
4. The children were found in a wretched house, a mere shed, near the river.
5. The girl who sang the national anthem is named Rebecca.
6. This is Mrs. Morgan, a member of the school committee.
7. My friend George is coming for a visit this weekend.

EXERCISE 26

1. The night **is** always darkest before the dawn.
2. Nothing **tastes** better than a grilled cheese sandwich.
3. Emily **admired** Katniss, so she **decided** to take archery lessons.
4. The dog **howled** as he **chased** the cat around the yard.

EXERCISE 27

Everything seemed strange when they went down. Hannah's familiar face looked unnatural as she flew about the kitchen. The big trunk stood ready in the hall, and mother's cloak and bonnet lay on the sofa. Nobody talked much, but as the time drew near, Mrs. March said to the girls: "Children, I leave you to Hannah's care. I have no fears for you. Go on with your work as usual, for work is a blessed solace."

EXERCISE 28

1. The children were playing on the seashore.
2. I will now write a letter.
3. I do not like his looks.
4. Do you hear your father?
5. Lost time is never found again.
6. Have you ever read *Robinson Crusoe*?
7. When does your birthday come?

EXERCISE 29

1. Who fed the Robin?
   past
2. We will expect you at noon.
   future
3. No mate, no comrade, Lucy knew.
   past
4. They are fighting for the cause of justice.
   present
5. They will fight for the cause of justice.
   future
6. They fought for the cause of justice.
   past
7. Father says no one will ever know why the ship sank.
   present
   future
   past

EXERCISE 30

1. The brook splashes and murmurs down the glen.
2. The boys fish in it all morning.

EXERCISE 31

PRESENT	PAST	PAST PARTICIPLE
beat	beat	beaten
begin	began	begun
bet	bet	bet
bite	bit	bitten
blow	blew	blown
break	broke	broken
bring	brought	brought
build	built	built
burst	burst	burst
buy	bought	bought
catch	caught	caught
choose	chose	chosen
cling	clung	clung
come	came	come
creep	crept	crept
dive	dived (dove)	dived
do	did	done
draw	drew	drawn
eat	ate	eaten
fall	fell	fallen
feel	felt	felt
fight	fought	fought
flee	fled	fled
fly	flew	flown
flow	flowed	flowed
forsake	forsook	forsaken
freeze	froze	frozen
get	got	got
give	gave	given
go	went	gone
grow	grew	grown
hide	hid	hidden
hurt	hurt	hurt
know	knew	known
lay	laid	laid
lie (recline)	lay	lain
lie (fib)	lied	lied
raise	raised	raised
ride	rode	ridden
ring	rang	rung
rise	rose	risen
run	ran	run
see	saw	seen
set	set	set
shake	shook	shaken
shine	shone	shone
show	showed	shown
shrink	shrank	shrunk
sing	sang	sung
sink	sank	sunk
sit	sat	sat
slay	slew	slain
sling	slung	slung

PRESENT	PAST	PAST PARTICIPLE
speak	spoke	spoken
spend	spent	spent
spring	sprang	sprung
steal	stole	stolen
stick	stuck	stuck
sting	stung	stung
strike	struck	struck
string	strung	strung
strive	strove	striven
swear	swore	sworn
swell	swelled	swollen
swim	swam	swum
swing	swung	swung
take	took	taken
teach	taught	taught
tear	tore	torn
throw	threw	thrown
thrust	thrust	thrust
tread	trod	trodden
wear	wore	worn
weave	wove	woven
weep	wept	wept
wet	wet	wet
win	won	won
wind	wound	wound
wring	wrung	wrung
write	wrote	written

EXERCISE 32

ASPECTS OF THE VERB "call"
Present: I **call**
Past: I **called**
Future: I will **call**
Present Perfect: I have **called**
Past Perfect: I had **called**
Future Perfect: I will have **called**

ASPECTS OF THE VERB "run"
Present: I **run**
Past: I **ran**
Future: I **will run**
Present Perfect: I **have run**
Past Perfect: I **had run**
Future Perfect: I **will have run**

ASPECTS OF THE VERB "sleep"
Present: I **sleep**
Past: I **slept**
Future: I **will sleep**
Present Perfect: I **have slept**
Past Perfect: I **had slept**
Future Perfect: I **will have slept**

ASPECTS OF THE VERB "play"
Present: I **play**
Past: I **played**
Future: I **will play**
Present Perfect: I **have played**
Past Perfect: I **had played**
Future Perfect: I **will have played**

EXERCISE 33

1. Katharine has just read that book.
   Present perfect
2. John will have finished it in an hour.
   Future perfect
3. He had nearly finished it before supper time.
   Past perfect
4. Where have you been all these years?
   Present perfect
5. I hope you will call often, now that you have returned.
   Present
   Future
   Present perfect
6. Many inventors had attempted flying machines before the Wrights built their successful airplane.
   Past perfect
   Past

EXERCISE 34

Present Progressive:	I am **writing**
Past Progressive:	I was **writing**
Future Progressive:	I will be **writing**
Present Perfect Progressive:	I have been **writing**
Past Perfect Progressive:	I had been **writing**
Future Perfect Progressive:	I will have been **writing**

Present Progressive:	I am **speaking**
Past Progressive:	I was **speaking**
Future Progressive:	I will be **speaking**
Present Perfect Progressive:	I have been **speaking**
Past Perfect Progressive:	I had been **speaking**
Future Perfect Progressive:	I will have been **speaking**

Present Progressive:	I **am working**
Past Progressive:	I **was working**
Future Progressive:	I **will be working**
Present Perfect Progressive:	I **have been working**
Past Perfect Progressive:	I **had been working**
Future Perfect Progressive:	I **will have been working**

EXERCISE 35

Answers will vary.

EXERCISE 36

1.	Mildred has been boating all morning.	present perfect progressive
2.	Do you enjoy boating?	present interrogative
3.	No, I do not enjoy it.	present negative
4.	I did enjoy it before our boating accident.	past emphatic
5.	Mildred and Elizabeth are reading now;	present progressive
	they will be eating lunch soon.	future progressive

EXERCISE 37

Past	Present Perfect	Past Perfect	Future Perfect
An oak **grew** at the gate.	It has grown for years.	It had grown for years.	It will have grown for years.
Tom **knew** the secret.	He has known it for a week.	He had known it for a week.	He will have known it for a week.
The boys **threw** the ball.	They have thrown it often.	They had thrown it often.	They will have thrown it often.
You **ate** the cake.	You have eaten every crumb.	You had eaten every crumb.	You will have eaten every crumb.
Fido **bit** the man.	He has bitten many people.	He had bitten many people.	He will have bitten many people.

EXERCISE 38

1. I frequently **lie** on the grass.
2. I have **lain** under that tree many times.
3. I have **laid** the book on the table.
4. Yesterday, the book **lay** on the table.
5. Chickens **lay** eggs.
6. That particular chicken has **laid** several eggs today.
7. He has **laid** his hat on the counter.
8. The book **lies** on the table now.
9. The book has **lain** on the table for a long time.
10. Please, **lay** the book down.

EXERCISE 39

1. The boy was **set** to work.
2. The sun **sets** in the west.
3. Have you **set** the supper table?
4. The doctor **set** the broken bone.
5. We **set** out early in the morning.
6. Do you **set** a good example?
7. The ring was **set** with jewels.
8. **Sit** in this chair.
9. The bird **sits** on her eggs.
10. The bird has **sat** on her eggs.

EXERCISE 40

1. The troops retired slowly.	Intransitive
2. Contractors build houses.	Transitive
3. I looked down from my window.	Intransitive
4. Matthew Henson explored the arctic.	Transitive
5. Benjamin Franklin invented stoves.	Transitive
6. The athletes jumped over the fence.	Intransitive

EXERCISE 41

Once upon a time the king of a large and rich country gathered together his army to take a faraway little country. The king and his soldiers marched all morning long then camped in the forest.

"Don't go today," said his landlord; "my wife bakes tomorrow, and she shall make you a cake."

Ivan headed for the door.

"Here," said the landlord, "here is a cake for you and your wife; and when you are most joyous together, then break the cake, but not sooner."

EXERCISE 42

1. The animals were fed by the farmer. Passive
The farmer fed the animals.
2. The farmers opened the flood gates. Active
The flood gates were opened by the farmers.
3. Mr. Long's house was destroyed by fire. Passive
The fire destroyed Mr. Long's house.
4. All grocers sell flour, tea, and coffee. Active
Flour, tea, and coffee are sold by all grocers.
5. Ichabod heard the barking of the watchdog. Active
The barking of the watchdog was heard by Ichabod.

EXERCISE 43

1. Boone lived alone until his brother returned.
2. Seals are killed when they are about four years old.
3. The hunter soon saw his mistake.
4. Franklin and his playmates used to fish for minnows in a mill pond.
5. I have not seen John and Charles since I met them at your house.
6. The birds use thread, which they themselves make from cotton.
7. Benedict Arnold, who was accused of treason, is infamous.

EXERCISE 44

1. He and (I) met at the gymnasium.
2. Her mother and (she) set out yesterday.
3. Did the teacher refer to you or (me)?
4. (We) boys are planning a sleigh ride.
5. (She) and Jane refused to go.
6. Luke was standing between John and (him).
7. (They) are the men we saw on the bridge.
8. (They) and (we) then hurried away.
9. (He) and (I) were feeding the squirrels.
10. Between you and (me), Richard is mistaken.
11. He gave it to Sophie and me.
12. The teacher and I modeled that map.
13. Louis and I have saved a dollar.
14. Caroline or I must stay at home.
15. Did you call mother or me?
16. When the man passed, the dogs barked at him.
17. Arthur whistled for his dog, but it did not come.
18. The schoolhouse had a large tree in front of it.
19. If James wants the book, let him have it.
20. The teacher asked his/her students to prepare their lessons.

EXERCISE 45

(adjectives in bold, nouns underlined, articles in italics)

1. *The* **yellow** flower glistened in *the* **hot summer** sun.
2. *The* **hungry** dog barked for **his** dinner. **(*)**
3. **Marley's seven** brothers grumbled when she asked to watch **her favorite princess** movie. **(*)**
4. Without warning, *the* **hot** flames turned *the* **wooden** door into ashes.
5. *A* majority of **middle school** students believed that *the* **math** final should be cancelled.

(*) *His* and *her* are possessive adjectives rather than possessive pronouns because they do not replace the noun.

EXERCISE 46

1. The clever burglar entered by the back door.
   descriptive; descriptive
2. The blue book belongs on the white shelf.
   descriptive; descriptive
3. Turn to the forty-third page.
   limiting
4. My new school has sixteen rooms.
   possessive; descriptive; limiting
5. The sailors escaped in two small boats.
   limiting; descriptive
6. The twelve jurors spent six weeks deliberating.
   limiting; limiting
7. That American flag is his flag.
   demonstrative, proper; possessive
8. The English knights fought to the death.
   proper

EXERCISE 47

Adjective	Comparative	Superlative
bad	worse	worst
big	bigger	biggest
boring	more boring	most boring
busy	busier	busiest
comfortable	more comfortable	most comfortable
cute	cuter	cutest
dirty	dirtier	dirtiest
dishonest	more dishonest	most dishonest
dry	drier (dryer)	driest (driest)
early	earlier	earliest
easy	easier	easiest
expensive	more expensive	most expensive
famous	more famous	most famous
fast	faster	fastest
friendly	friendlier	friendliest
generous	more generous	most generous
gloomy	gloomier	gloomiest
good	better	best
healthy	healthier	healthiest
high	higher	highest
honest	more honest	most honest
hot	hotter	hottest
interesting	more interesting	most interesting
kind	kinder	kindest
large	larger	largest
little	less	least
long	longer	longest
many	more	most
much	more	most
nice	nicer	nicest
pretty	prettier	prettiest
quiet	quieter	quietest
sad	sadder	saddest
safe	safer	safest
short	shorter	shortest
terrific	more terrific	most terrific
wise	wiser	wisest
young	younger	youngest

EXERCISE 48

1. Apples were scattered everywhere.	scattered
2. The officers handled the men roughly.	handled
3. Mr. Smith formerly lived there.	lived
	lived
4. The sun rose pleasantly on the village.	rose
5. The horse suddenly ran away.	ran
	ran
6. You all did love him once.	love
7. A light, swift boat sped northward.	sped

EXERCISE 49

1. lazy	lazily
2. remarkable	remarkably
3. angry	angrily

EXERCISE 50

1. The large sailboat (in the harbor) was anchored (by the opening) (of the bay).
2. (After dinner), we can roast marshmallows (over the fire).
3. My brother likes skateboarding (at the skate park) (with his friends).
4. (On my way), I will stop (at the store) (for groceries).
5. (In the store window), you can see all the items (for sale).

EXERCISE 51

1. When Benjamin Franklin was seventeen, he ran away from his home in Boston.
2. He first went to New York on a sailing vessel.
3. Not finding work, he started on foot to Philadelphia.
4. When he got there, his clothes were spattered with mud, and under each arm, he carried a long roll of bread that he had just bought.
5. A girl named Deborah Read laughed at him as he trudged along the street, but a few years after this, she became his wife.

EXERCISE 52

1. For further particulars, inquire *within.*	adverb
2. Mr. Hatch will return *within* an hour.	preposition
3. The boy ran *up* the hill.	preposition
4. Run *up* the flag.	adverb
5. The carpenter fell *off* the house.	preposition
6. Suddenly, one of the wheels came *off.*	adverb
7. We shall come back *before* dinner.	preposition
8. I have seen that man *before.*	adverb
9. He turned *on* the alarm.	adverb
10. The dog stood *on* the grass.	preposition

EXERCISE 53

1. Georgia and Alabama produce much cotton.
2. George Washington was skillful but cautious.
3. We stayed because the weather was stormy.
4. La Salle was a bold and tireless explorer.
5. He sailed up the lake and down the river.
6. He kept on though it was cold and stormy.
7. Men never succeed unless they try.
8. I will talk with you, but I will not eat with you.
9. The earth was bright, and the sky was blue.
10. Do you intend to be a lawyer or a doctor?

EXERCISE 54

1. Will school open on Monday or Tuesday?
2. Fred went fishing, but he caught nothing.
3. Christmas came, so school was closed.
4. The hammer has been lost or stolen.
5. It rained very hard, but I had an umbrella.
6. Shall I boil or bake the potatoes?
7. Clara finished her work and went out to play.
8. Who found the bracelet, Anna or Emily?
9. Are the apples in the house or in the barn?
10. He will arrive soon if the plane isn't late.

EXERCISE 55

Answers will vary concerning feelings expressed.

1. Pshaw! That's no reason.
   impatience or exasperation
2. Alas! What will become of me now!
   hopelessness
3. Oh my goodness, what will she say to this?
   surprise
4. Hooray! I've caught a fish!
   joy
5. Oh! I'm thankful he is gone!
   frustration
6. Aye, tear down her horrible sign!
   anger
7. Oh that the waves were flowing over me!
   sadness
8. O Father! I hear the sound of fireworks.
   excitement
9. Goodbye! Come again soon!
   affection
10. Help! Somebody help me!
   fear

EXERCISE 56

1. Fleming | awoke (at six o'clock).
2. Her eyes | twinkle (like a star).
3. The bread | browned (in the oven).
4. Our dance class | practiced (for our instructor).
5. The baseball team | played until the sun went down. (*Until* can act as a preposition or a conjunction signaling a dependent clause. *Until the sun went down* is a dependent clause. *Sun* is the subject. *Went* is the verb.)

EXERCISE 57

1. James Fennimore Cooper | wrote adventure stories.
2. The poet Whittier | once taught school.
3. | Do not trouble him.
4. They | want him and me.
5. |Study the material for your test tomorrow.

EXERCISE 58

1. Pizarro, a Spanish adventurer, conquered Peru.
   Pattern 2
2. The traveler departed without delay.
   Pattern 1
3. The lilacs bloomed in the backyard.
   Pattern 1
4. Put away your books.
   Pattern 2
5. In the Sahara, the date trees blossom in April.
   Pattern 1

EXERCISE 59

1. Some men | are generous.
2. The weather | is cold!
3. | Do not look so cross.
4. The room | seems damp.
5. His gallant horse | was dead.
6. I | am terribly anxious.
7. November woods | are bare.
8. He | became too careless.
9. He | appears very much discouraged.
10. The air | has grown very misty.

EXERCISES 60

Answers will vary.
Ensure the adjectives come at the end of the sentence and follow intransitive verbs, often linking verbs.

EXERCISES 61

Answers will vary.
Ensure that the nouns used are properly labeled predicate nouns, and the adjectives used are properly labeled predicate adjectives.

EXERCISES 62

Answers will vary.
Ensure that these nouns fall at the ends of the sentences and offer another word for the subject.

EXERCISE 63

(Indirect objects are marked in bold type.)
1. I paid the **cashier** fifty dollars.
2. Who taught **you** grammar?
3. The usher handed each **visitor** a program.
4. Thrice they offered **him** a kingly crown.
5. I built my **grandmother** a beautiful house.
6. Franklin rendered the **colonies** a great service.
7. O, give **me** my lowly thatched cottage again.
8. His mother gave **him** pocket money.
9. Constant success only shows **us** one side of life.
10. Do not lend **him** money.

EXERCISE 64

1. The umpire decided the game lost.	adjective
2. Everybody thought him insane.	adjective
3. He painted his house white.	adjective
4. Do you consider your friend a poet?	noun
5. He makes me angry.	adjective
6. I count my health my greatest wealth.	noun
7. They named their daughter Tuesdae.	noun

EXERCISE 65

1. The horse is black.	Pattern 3
2. My head aches.	Pattern 1
3. Do not touch me.	Pattern 2
4. The fishermen caught nothing.	Pattern 2
5. Tadpoles become frogs.	Pattern 3
6. They disappeared.	Pattern 1
7. The bird died.	Pattern 1
8. Glass feels smooth.	Pattern 3
9. You seem weary.	Pattern 3
10. Do not trouble him.	Pattern 2

EXERCISE 66

1. The lady *in the black dress* was Mrs. Robinson.
phrase
2. The lady *who wore the black dress* was Mrs. Robinson. clause
3. Please return the book *that you borrowed.*
clause
4. A dog *that is always barking* does not often bite.
clause
5. The evil *that men do* lives after them.
clause
6. The man *who married Pocahontas* was John Rolfe.
clause
7. People *who are lazy* often take the most pains.
clause
8. We took the road *that led directly* to New Haven.
clause
9. *When the gate opened,* the procession filed in.
clause
10. Where is the house *whose chimney was blown down*? clause

EXERCISE 67

1. The man who hesitates is lost.
man
2. This is the house that Jack built.
house
3. Am I the person to whom you refer?
person
4. I know the place where the strawberries grow.
place
5. The tiger is a beast that kills without pity.
beast
6. Nobody wants a farm that produces no crops.
farm
7. Is that the man whose house was burned?
man
8. Evils that cannot be cured must be endured.
evils
9. The only jewel which will not decay is knowledge.
jewel
10. I remember the lilacs where the robins nested.
lilacs

EXERCISE 68

Answers will vary. Possible responses:
1. who are sick
2. that I lent you.
3. that you gave me.
4. that was down in the basement?
5. which wasn't paved.
6. who don't pass their classes

EXERCISE 69

Answers will vary. Possible responses:
1. We took a drive after we ate dinner.
2. Few men are idle when times are good.
3. When I return, I will read you the letter.
4. Do you errands before you go to school.
5. Some boys talked while Mr. Brown was lecturing.

EXERCISE 70

1. Strike while the iron is hot.
2. Make hay while the sun shines.
3. Be silent that you may hear.
4. Fools rush in where angels fear to tread.
5. Caesar had a fever when he was in Spain.
6. Smooth runs the water where the brook is deep.
7. William Cullen Bryant wrote poetry when he was a boy.
8. The raft went very well until it met a swift current.
9. Childhood shows the man as morning shows the day.
10. If a man empties his purse into his head, no one can take it away from him.

EXERCISE 71

1. He thinks that I am mistaken.
   object
2. That he speaks the truth is certain.
   subject
3. Every man ate what he wanted.
   object
4. How you do it is a mystery to me.
   subject
5. That Mrs. Hanson won is now acknowledged.
   subject

EXERCISE 72

Answers will vary. Possible responses:
1. I predict that the weather will change.
2. He promised he would reply early.
3. Everything indicates we will have a cold winter.
4. The jury believed the man was guilty.
5. We expect business will improve.

EXERCISE 73

1. He knew that the car was broken.
   direct object
2. His promise was that he would return soon.
   predicate noun
3. The jury believed that the woman was guilty.
   direct object
4. My expectation is that my brother will arrive today.
   predicate noun
5. That the earth is round can be easily shown.
   subject
6. The probability is that it will rain tomorrow.
   predicate noun
7. Many believe that the soul is immortal.
   direct object
8. I dream that everyone might live free.
   direct object

EXERCISE 74

1. Little Jack Horner sat (in a corner.)
Sat where? adv
2. Jack and Jill went (up the hill.)
Went where? adv
3. My brother will return (in two weeks.)
Return when? adv
4. The dial (on this radio) is broken.
Which dial? adj
5. The chairs (on the veranda) are new.
Which chairs? adj
6. That woman works (with great energy.)
Works how? adv

EXERCISE 75

1. Who is that girl with the dark eyes?
2. Jackson was a man of courage.
3.Some pets can learn with ease.

EXERCISE 76

1. My sister wants to shop after school.
   infinitive
2. Shopping is her favorite hobby.
   gerund
3. The melting candle dripped on the tablecloth.
   participle
4. I have no one to decorate the gym with me.
   infinitive
5. The exhausted children napped on the floor.
   participle

EXERCISE 77

1. Helping prepare dinner will make your family happy. gerund phrase
2. Setting the table is a great start.
   gerund phrase
3. My family likes to cook together.
   infinitive phrase
4. We watch my dad grilling in the backyard.
   participial phrase
5. To make a salad, my mom gathers vegetables from our garden. infinitive phrase

EXERCISE 78

1. I saw her singing at her work.
   present
2. Hannah is at the window binding shoes.
   present
3. Truth crushed to earth shall rise again.
   past
4. Circling above us, the black rooks fly.
   present
5. It is dangerous to live in a house built of glass.
   past
6. The deer saw the boat headed for her.
   past
7. 'Tis the last rose of summer, left blooming alone.
   past
8. Having seen the giant, the man was afraid.
   perfect
9. Often I sat in my room reading the greater part of the night. present
10. The children coming home from school look in at the open door. present

EXERCISE 79

1. Giving is better than receiving.
   To give is better than to receive.
2. Walking several miles a day would do you good.
   To walk several miles a day would do you good.
3. Knowing some trade is a great convenience.
   To know some trade is a great convenience.
4. I shall continue to study arithmetic.
   I shall continue studying arithmetic.
5. Do you like writing essays?
   Do you like to write essays?

EXERCISE 80

1. They love to see the flaming forge.
   object
2. To copy a whole page is rather tiresome.
   subject
3. To waste valuable time is unwise.
   subject
4. The carpenter decided to do the work alone.
   object
5. I now tried to sit up and paddle the boat.
   object
6. To escape from poverty is no easy matter.
   subject
7. I want to fly the plane by myself.
   object
8. I attempted to land upon the Cape of the Woods.
   object

EXERCISE 81

1. Hooray, I found my laptop!
2. My hand trembles.
3. Is your name Jacob?
4. Get away from the ledge!
5. Sugar tastes sweet.
6. Oh no, the tire is flat!
7. Will you have some?
8. Turn off your phones.
9. Are you finished with the job?
10. Help me!

EXERCISE 82

1. I envy a person who can speak two languages, play an instrument, and cook a gourmet meal.
2. Before you go to school, get dressed, eat breakfast, and brush your teeth.
3. The marching band played during halftime, and the cheerleaders performed, too.
4. After the war ended, Washington retired to Mt. Vernon.
5. Dad, may I go to the mall?
6. Take your own time, Annie.
7. Come into the garden, Maud.
8. Do your very best, my child, each day of your life.

EXERCISE 83

1. Stephen likes salad; Jennifer likes chocolate.
2. I put off completing my homework; therefore, I was unprepared for the quiz.
3. My brother plays the violin; I play the piano.
4. I need to travel to Los Angeles, California; Dallas, Texas; and Miami, Florida.
5. Ted wanted to play baseball; however, he had to take care of his dog.
6. Jonathan plays the piano; he wants to play the clarinet.
7. The test was extremely difficult; however, I had studied for it.
8. I plan to run a marathon next month; therefore, I need to exercise more frequently.
9. The movie was amazing; I fell asleep, however, before the ending.
10. Oscar the cat is adorable; however, he is very mischievous.

EXERCISE 84

1. "No other tree is as wonderful as I am," said the pine tree.
2. "Be sure, my child," said the widow to her little daughter, "that you always do just as you are told."
3. "Why did you not lay up food during the summer?" inquired the ant of the grasshopper.
4. "But it is so delightful to swim about in the water," said the duckling.
5.

Once upon a time, a little leaf was heard to sigh and cry, as leaves often do when a gentle wind is about, and the twig said, "What is the matter, little leaf?"

The leaf said, "The wind has just told me that one day it would pull me off and throw me down on the ground to wither."

6. "I am not a bird, but a mouse," said the bat.
7. Emerson said, "Light is the best policeman."
8. "I would rather be right than be President," said Henry Clay.

EXERCISE 85

1. “Where do you live?” asked the stranger of Alice.	direct
2. “Don’t fail, boys,” said Matthew, “to come over this evening.”	direct
3. We asked John where he was going so early.	indirect
4. “Get ready!” cried Standish to his men.	direct
5. The paper says that the weather will be colder tomorrow.	indirect
6. Tony exclaimed, "I am ready."	direct
7. Robert exclaimed that he was ready, too.	indirect
8. Margaret said, “I will come."	direct
9. The other students said that they would come.	indirect
10. Mother asked me, "Did you clean your room?"	direct

EXERCISE 86

Amsterdam, Holland
November 8, 1899

Dear Boys,

I wonder whether you miss me as much as I miss you. I wish you were here in Amsterdam with us, for it is a beautiful city, and it is full of curious sights. Mrs. Lynch has bought a pair of Dutch wooden shoes to take to little Leigh, and I have bought a funny old Dutch watch.

Tonight we go to London, and in the morning we shall be in the rooms where you were with us ten days ago. I shall expect to hear from each one of you once a week. Meanwhile be courteous and attentive to Professor and Madame Ruhle; when you play, play hard, when you study, study hard. You must take good care of your health, and be careful not to over exert yourself at the gymnasium. Pinny must write to his Aunt Etta, Melvin must write to Mr. Gray, and sometimes Dady must write to his Aunt Carrie. On the other side are the office addresses. Good-bye, my dear boys; I shall write again from London in a day or two.

Affectionately,
Eugene Field.

Made in the USA
San Bernardino, CA
27 August 2019